CW01011013

Microsoft V

explained

Books Available

By the same authors: *acces ?*

BP585	Microsoft Excel 2007 explained
BP584	Microsoft Word 2007 explained ✓
BP583	Microsoft Office 2007 explained
BP581	Windows Vista explained
BP580	Windows Vista for Beginners
BP569	Microsoft Works 8.0 & Works Suite 2006 explained
BP563	Using Windows XP's Accessories
BP558	Microsoft Works 8.0 & Works Suite 2005 explained
BP557	How Did I Do That ... in Windows XP
BP555	Using PDF Files
BP550	Advanced Guide to Windows XP
BP548	Easy PC Keyboard Shortcuts
BP546	Microsoft Works Suite 2004 explained
BP545	Paint Shop Pro 8 explained
BP544	Microsoft Office 2003 explained
BP538	Windows XP for Beginners
BP525	Controlling Windows XP the easy way
BP522	Microsoft Works Suite 2002 explained
BP514	Windows XP explained
BP513	IE 6 and Outlook Express 6 explained
BP512	Microsoft Access 2002 explained
BP511	Microsoft Excel 2002 explained
BP510	Microsoft Word 2002 explained
BP509	Microsoft Office XP explained
BP498	Using Visual Basic
BP493	Windows Me explained
BP491	Windows 2000 explained
BP487	Quicken 2000 UK explained
BP486	Using Linux the easy way
BP465	Lotus SmartSuite Millennium explained
BP433	Your own Web site on the Internet
BP341	MS-DOS explained
BP284	Programming in QuickBASIC
BP258	Learning to Program in C

589 Pent ppt presentation with Power Point 2007 Boben

614 Computing with Vista for the older generation

Microsoft Word 2007 explained

by

P.R.M. Oliver
and
N. Kantaris

Bernard Babani (publishing) Ltd
The Grampians
Shepherds Bush Road
London W6 7NF
England
www.babanibooks.com

Please Note

Although every care has been taken with the production of this book to ensure that any projects, designs, modifications and/or programs, etc., contained herewith, operate in a correct and safe manner and also that any components specified are normally available in Great Britain, the Publishers and Author(s) do not accept responsibility in any way for the failure (including fault in design) of any project, design, modification or program to work correctly or to cause damage to any equipment that it may be connected to or used in conjunction with, or in respect of any other damage or injury that may be so caused, nor do the Publishers accept responsibility in any way for the failure to obtain specified components.

Notice is also given that if equipment that is still under warranty is modified in any way or used or connected with home-built equipment then that warranty may be void.

First Published - October 2007

British Library Cataloguing in Publication Data:

A catalogue record for this book is available from the British Library

ISBN 978 0 085934 584 2

Cover Design by Gregor Arthur
Printed and Bound by J. H. Haynes & Co. Ltd., Sparkford

About this Package

Microsoft Word 2007 explained has been written to help users to get to grips with Microsoft's new word processor *Word* 2007, part of the *Microsoft Office 2007* package, specifically designed for both the *Windows Vista* and *Windows XP* environments.

Microsoft Word 2007 is an exciting new program that will help with the new demands, challenges and opportunities to individuals and business. It has a completely new interface which replaces the menus, toolbars and most of the task panes and dialogue boxes of previous versions, with a ribbon of buttons organised into themed tabs, a Quick Access toolbar that you can customise with commands you use the most, and just one menu.

The package incorporates several new features, as well as improvements on its previous capabilities. These improvements include:

- The new Ribbon in Word 2007 groups tools by task, and the commands you use most frequently are close at hand. This new, results-oriented interface presents tools to you when you need them.

- The ability to do your blogging from Word.

- You now get a live visual preview of the formatting in your document before you actually make a change.

- New chart and diagram features include three-dimensional shapes, transparency, drop shadows, and other effects.

- Quick Styles and Document Themes let you quickly change the appearance of text, tables, and graphics throughout your document.

- Word 2007 lets you export your files in either PDF (Portable Document Format) or XPS format, but you need extra software to do this.

No previous knowledge is assumed, but the book does not describe how to install and use Microsoft Windows itself. If you need to know more about Windows, then may we suggest you select a book from the 'Books Available' list published by BERNARD BABANI (publishing) Ltd.

Microsoft Word 2007 explained was written using both Windows Vista and Windows XP. The only real differences, as far as the book is concerned, being that Vista's **Start** menu does not cascade, its window frames, by default, are semi transparent, and it uses Vista's newly designed system dialogue boxes.

This book introduces Word 2007 with sufficient detail to get you working, then discusses how to use the built-in Internet features – especially the new **blogging** tools, how to share information between programs, and how to get started with macros. No prior knowledge of the package's capabilities is assumed.

The book was written with the busy person in mind. It is not necessary to learn all there is to know about a subject, when reading a few selected pages can usually do the same thing quite adequately. With the help of this book, it is hoped that you will be able to come to terms with Microsoft Word 2007 and get the most out of your computer in terms of efficiency, productivity and enjoyment, and that you will be able to do it in the shortest, most effective and informative way.

About the Authors

Phil Oliver graduated in Mining Engineering at Camborne School of Mines in 1967 and since then has specialised in most aspects of surface mining technology, with a particular emphasis on computer related techniques. He has worked in Guyana, Canada, several Middle Eastern and Asian countries, South Africa and the United Kingdom, on such diverse projects as: the planning and management of bauxite, iron, gold and coal mines; rock excavation contracting in the UK; international mining equipment sales and international mine consulting. In 1988 he took up a lecturing position at Camborne School of Mines (part of Exeter University) in Surface Mining and Management. He retired from this in 1998, to spend more time writing, consulting and developing Web sites for clients.

Noel Kantaris graduated in Electrical Engineering at Bristol University and after spending three years in the Electronics Industry in London, took up a Tutorship in Physics at the University of Queensland. Research interests in Ionospheric Physics, led to the degrees of M.E. in Electronics and Ph.D. in Physics. On return to the UK, he took up a Post-Doctoral Research Fellowship in Radio Physics at the University of Leicester, and then in 1973 a lecturing position in Engineering at the Camborne School of Mines, Cornwall, (part of Exeter University), where between 1978 and 1997 he was also the CSM IT Manager. At present he is IT Director of FFC Ltd.

Acknowledgements

We would like to thank friends and colleagues, for their helpful tips and suggestions which assisted us in the writing of this book.

Trademarks

Arial and **Times New Roman** are registered trademarks of The Monotype Corporation plc.

HP and LaserJet are registered trademarks of Hewlett Packard Corporation.

IBM is a registered trademark of International Business Machines, Inc.

Intel is a registered trademark of Intel Corporation.

Calibri, **Cambria**, **Excel**, **IntelliMouse**, **Microsoft**, **MS-DOS**, **Office logo**, **Outlook**, **PowerPoint**, **SmartArt**, **Visual Basic** and **Windows**, are either registered trademarks or trademarks of Microsoft Corporation.

PostScript is a registered trademark of Adobe Systems Incorporated.

TrueType is a registered trademark of Apple Corporation.

All other brand and product names and logos used in the book are recognised as trademarks, or registered trademarks, of their respective companies.

Contents

1

Package Overview

Microsoft's Word 2007 is part of the Office 2007 package and is without doubt the best Windows word processor so far. As you would expect, it is fully integrated with all the other Office 2007 applications. Like previous versions of Word, it has particularly strong leanings towards desk top publishing which offers fully editable WYSIWYG (what you see is what you get) modes that can be viewed in various screen views and zoom levels. Couple this with the ability to include, manipulate and even edit full colour graphics and to easily create chart and diagram features, include three-dimensional shapes, transparency, drop shadows, and other effects and you can see the enormous power of the program.

Once you get used to the new interface, you will find using Word 2007 to be even more intuitive and easy than earlier versions and you will soon be producing the type of word processed output you would not have dreamt possible.

In many situations Word 2007 will attempt to anticipate what you want to do and will probably produce the correct result most of the time. For example, AutoCorrect and AutoFormat can, when active, correct common spelling mistakes and format documents automatically. Other Wizards can help you with everyday tasks and/or make complex tasks easier to manage.

Word 2007 uses Object Linking and Embedding (OLE) to move and share information seamlessly between Office applications. For example, you can drag information from one application to another, or you can link information from one application into another.

Finally, writing macros in Visual Basic gives you a powerful development platform with which to create custom solutions.

The New 2007 Interface

Word 2007 has a built-in consistency with the other applications that make up Office 2007 which makes them easier to use. Previous releases used a system of menus, toolbars, task panes, and dialogue boxes to access commands and get things done.

Because 2007 programs do so much more, these features have been replaced with a new user interface which makes it easier to find and use the full range of features they provide. This is somewhat daunting at first, but once you start using the new interface you will very rapidly get used to it. We did anyway!

The Ribbon

Traditional menus and toolbars have been replaced by the Ribbon – a new device that presents commands organised into a set of tabs.

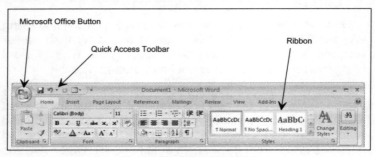

Fig. 1.1 The Word 2007 Ribbon

The tabs on the Ribbon display the commands that are most relevant for each of the task areas in the applications, as shown above. Contextual tabs also appear when they are needed so that you can very easily find and use the commands needed for the current operation. As an example, clicking on a picture in a document in Word 2007, opens a contextual tab on the Ribbon with commands used for editing a picture. Once you leave the picture, this tab disappears.

Fig. 1.1 on the previous page also shows two of the other new features of Word 2007. These are:

The Microsoft Office Button

 The Microsoft Office Button (or **Office Button** as we shall call it), replaces the **File** menu of previous versions and is located in the upper-left corner of the Word window.

When you click this button you see commands to **Open**, **Save**, **Send** and **Print** your file, as well as new commands such as **Finish** and **Publish**. The right side of the menu lists your recently opened documents, and gives access to the application's control options.

Quick Access Toolbar

The Quick Access Toolbar is the small area to the upper left of the Ribbon, as shown in Fig. 1.1. This bar contains buttons for the things that you use over and over every day, such as **Save**, **Undo**, and **Repeat**. It is very easy to add your favourite commands to it so that they are available no matter which tab you are on.

These and the other new features of the Word 2007 user interface are described in more detail in the next chapter.

How to Get Classic Menus

If you really can't come to terms with the new 2007 interface, there is at least one way to get the classic menus and toolbars back, as an add-in which you can download from:

www.addintools.com/english/menuword/

We haven't done it ourselves, but you can download and install this software and "you will see and enjoy the classic menu and toolbars of Word 2003 or Word XP in Word 2007". At less than £10.00 it could be worth a try.

Hardware and Software Requirements

Word 2007 is part of Microsoft Office 2007, so if this is already installed on your computer, you can safely skip this and the next section of this chapter.

The minimum requirements for Office 2007 are an IBM-compatible PC with a processor of at least 500 MHz, (1 gigahertz (GHz) processor or higher for Outlook with Business Contact Manager), 256 MB of RAM and 2 GB of hard disc space. 512 MB of RAM or higher is recommended for Outlook with Business Contact Manager. Some of the hard disc space will be freed after installation if the original download package is removed from the hard drive.

In addition you will require:

- Microsoft Windows XP with Service Pack (SP) 2, Windows Server 2003 with SP1, or later operating system (such as Windows Vista).

- A CD-ROM or DVD drive.

- 1024x768 or higher resolution monitor.

- Connectivity to Microsoft Exchange Server 2000 or later is required for certain advanced functionality in Outlook 2007. Connectivity to Microsoft Windows Server 2003 with SP1 or later running Microsoft Windows SharePoint Services is required for certain advanced collaboration functionality. Microsoft Office SharePoint Server 2007 is required for certain advanced functionality. As far as this book is concerned, none of these are required!

- To share data among multiple computers, the host computer must be running Windows Server 2003 with SP1, Windows XP Professional with SP2, or later.

- Microsoft Internet Explorer 6.0 or later, 32-bit browser only.

- Internet functionality requires access to the Internet.

Downloading Office 2007

Perhaps the easiest way to get started with Office 2007 is to download a free trial version from the following Web address:

http://ukireland.trymicrosoftoffice.com/

For us this opened the window shown in Fig. 1.2 below.

Fig. 1.2 Downloading a Version of Office 2007

We clicked the button against Microsoft® Office Professional 2007 and had to log in to Windows Live ID. Once this was done the download page was presented. We made a note of the Microsoft Office Product Key and clicked both the **Download** buttons, choosing to save the files to a new folder on our hard drive.

The downloads, at 635MB, were very large and took time enough for a shower and several mugs of coffee, but our selected folder then contained two new files.

- X12-30196.exe – This was 388 MB and contained the 2007 Office suite.

- X13-11296.exe – This was 247 MB and only contained the Business Contact Manager add-in.

Trial Conditions

To start a trial, once you have installed it (as described in the next section) you must activate the trial software over the Internet. The activation process begins automatically when you open any Microsoft Office 2007 product for the first time. If you prefer, you can bypass the activation and launch Office 2007 applications up to 25 times before you need to enter the Product Key and activate the package.

Before the trial period ends you will start receiving reminders saying when the trial will end. If you click the **Convert** button in one of these message windows, you can convert your trial software to the full licensed version in the Setup Wizard that opens. In the Setup dialogue box, click **Enter Product Key** if you have bought the full product from a retailer, or click **Buy Online Key** if you do not have a perpetual product key and would like to purchase it online.

With the first option, to avoid having to uninstall the trial version and then reinstall the full version make sure that you purchase the same full product version and language as the trial software you used.

After the trial period ends, if you do not buy Office 2007, you can still use the trial version after a fashion, but with the following limitations:

- You will not be able to create any new files.

- You will not be able to modify existing files.

- You will be able to print existing files but not save them.

After launching the full version for the first time you will need to activate it. You can do this over the Internet or by phone. The default option is to activate the software over the Internet. The trial is then converted to perpetual use with no uninstall or reinstall necessary. Good luck!

Installing Microsoft Office 2007

Installing Office on your computer's hard disc is now a fairly painless operation. If you are installing the trial version, locate the file **X12-30196.exe** that you downloaded onto your hard disc, and double-click on it to start the set-up process. Be aware though, that you may have downloaded a different file name, so make sure you make a note of it.

To install Microsoft Office from the box, place the distribution CD in your CD/DVD drive and close it. The auto-start program on the CD should start the SETUP

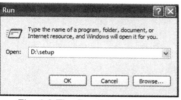

Fig. 1.3 The Run Dialogue Box

program automatically. If it doesn't, click the **Start** button, and select the **Run** command which opens the Run dialogue box, as shown in Fig. 1.3. Next, type in the **Open** box:

```
D:\setup
```

In our case the CD/DVD was the d: drive; yours could be different. Clicking the **OK** button, starts the installation of Microsoft Office 2007. With both methods, SETUP first displays a message box telling you it is extracting files and then opens the Enter your Product Key window, shown in Fig. 1.4 below.

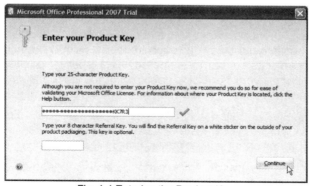

Fig. 1.4 Entering the Product Key

From now on you just follow the instructions given. If you don't enter the Product Key code correctly you will not be able to go further though! Clicking the **Continue** button opens the next window for you to read and accept Microsoft's licence terms.

In the next window, click **Install Now** for a default complete installation of Office 2007, or click **Customize** which gives you some choices.

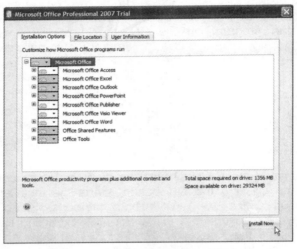

Fig. 1.5 The Installation Options Window

The Installation Options tab, shown open above, lists the Office 2007 applications to be installed and how they will run. You work your way through this list until the type of installation you want is selected. The space required and available on your hard disc is shown in the bottom right of the pane.

The File Location tab lets you set where on your hard disc(s) Office will be installed. The User Information tab lets you enter or change your name, initials and company.

Clicking the **Install Now** button, pointed to above, copies files to your computer's hard disc, sets up the applications and hopefully displays the window shown in Fig. 1.6.

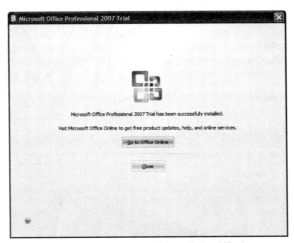

Fig. 1.6 The Successful Installation Window

To start an Office 2007 application in Windows XP, use the **Start**, **All Programs** command and select the **Microsoft Office** entry from the menu, as shown in Fig. 1.7.

Fig. 1.7 The Microsoft Office Cascade Menu

Clicking on one of the Office applications starts the Activation Wizard. During activation, the product ID and a non-unique hardware identification are sent to Microsoft, but it does not include personal information or any data held on your computer. The product ID is generated from the product key used to install the software and a generic code representing the version and language of the Microsoft Office being activated. The non-unique hardware identification represents the configuration of your PC at the time of activation.

The hardware identification identifies only the PC and is used solely for the purpose of activation. Office can detect and accept changes to your PC configuration. Minor upgrades will not require re-activation, however, if you completely overhaul your PC, you may be required to activate your product again.

The first Office 2007 Activation Wizard screen is shown in Fig. 1.8 below.

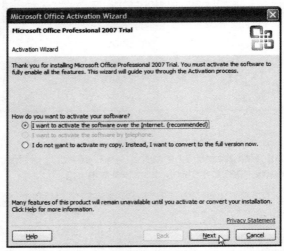

Fig. 1.8 The Office Activation Wizard Screen

As you can see, in this Wizard screen you would normally be able to choose the method of activation; via the Internet, or by telephone. In our case above, we were activating a trial copy so the telephone option was greyed out and not available. If you choose to activate your product through the Internet and you are not already connected, the Wizard will help you get connected.

Note: There is no software registration with the 2007 Office system. Instead, you have the option of registering for special online services from Microsoft Office Online. These include free community-submitted templates and search results tailored to the products you have installed.

Adding or Removing Office Applications

Fig. 1.9 The Windows Start Menu

To add or remove an Office application with Windows XP, left-click the *start* button and click the **Control Panel** option on the Windows pop-up menu, as shown in Fig. 1.9. This opens the Control Panel dialogue box shown in Fig. 1.10.

Next, double-click the **Add/Remove Programs** icon, pointed to in Fig. 1.10 (or **Programs and Features** in Vista) to open the Add or Remove Programs dialogue box shown in Figure 1.11 on the next page.

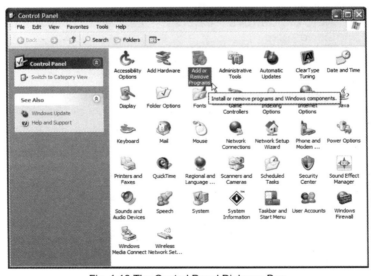

Fig. 1.10 The Control Panel Dialogue Box

Next, locate the Microsoft Office program and click the **Change** button, as shown for Windows XP below. In Windows Vista the **Change** option is in the command bar above the program listing.

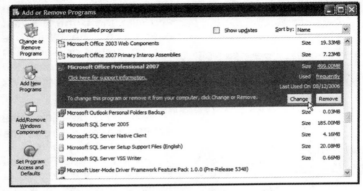

Fig. 1.11 The Add/Remove Programs Dialogue Box

This opens a simple window with options for you to change your installation of Office 2007.

- **Add or Remove Features** – Lets you change your Office setup.

- **Repair** – Reinstalls the whole of Office 2007 to fix any errors in the original installation.

- **Remove** – Uninstalls Office 2007 from your system.
  In Vista the **Uninstall** option is in the command bar above the program listing.

- **Convert** – Available for the Trial version to let you easily convert to the final version.

Selecting the **Add or Remove Features** option and pressing the **Continue** button opens up the dialogue box of Fig. 1.12 on the facing page.

This is similar to the one used for an initial custom installation, shown in Fig. 1.5, but without the options to control the saving destination or your personal information.

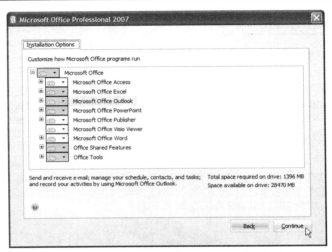

Fig. 1.12 The Installation Options for Office Applications

A plus (+) sign to the left of an application indicates sub-features which you can add or remove from the Office installation by right-clicking it and selecting from the list of options that appear, as shown in Fig. 1.13 below.

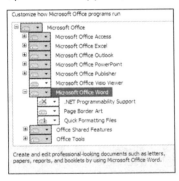

Fig. 1.13 Setting Options
for Office Applications

Run from My Computer will install and store a feature on your hard disc. **Run all from My Computer** will also install and store all the sub-features. With **Installed on First Use** the feature will be installed on your hard disc when you use it for the first time. Selecting **Not Available** will remove the feature.

The Mouse Pointers

In Word 2007, as with all other graphical based programs, using a mouse makes many operations both easier and more fun to carry out.

The program makes use of the mouse pointers available in Windows, some of the most common of which are illustrated below. When an Office application is initially started up the first you will see is the hourglass with Windows XP, or the rotating circle with Windows Vista, which turns into an upward pointing hollow arrow once the individual application screen appears on your display. Other shapes depend on the type of work you are doing at the time.

The rotating Vista circle which displays when you are waiting while performing a function.

The XP hourglass which displays when you are waiting while performing a function.

The arrow which appears when the pointer is placed over menus, scrolling bars, and buttons.

The I-beam which appears in normal text areas of the screen. For additional 'Click and Type' pointer shapes, specific to Word, see the table overleaf.

The 4-headed arrow which appears when you choose to move a table, a chart area, or a frame.

The double arrows which appear when over the border of a window, used to drag the side and alter the size of the window.

The Help hand which appears in the Help windows, and is used to access 'hypertext' type links.

Office 2007 applications, like other Windows packages, have additional mouse pointers which facilitate the execution of selected commands. Some of these are:

The vertical pointer which appears when pointing over a column in a table or worksheet and used to select the column.

The horizontal pointer which appears when pointing at a row in a table or worksheet and used to select the row.

The slanted arrow which appears when the pointer is placed in the selection bar area of text or a table.

The vertical split arrow which appears when pointing over the area separating two columns and used to size a column.

The horizontal split arrow which appears when pointing over the area separating two rows and used to size a row.

+   The cross which you drag to extend or fill a series.

The draw pointer which appears when you are drawing freehand.

Word 2007 also has the following Click and Type pointer shapes which appear as you move the I-beam pointer into a specific formatting zone; their shape indicating which formatting will apply when you double-click.

I⁼	Align left	⁼I	Align right
I	Centre	I⁼	Left indent
I⁼	Left text wrap	⁼I	Right text wrap

Fig. 1.14 The Click and Type Pointer Shapes in Word 2007

If you don't see the Click and Type pointer shapes, check that the facility is turned on. You do this by clicking the **Word Options** button in the Microsoft Button menu, then clicking the Advanced tab and selecting the **Enable click and type** check box.

Getting Help in Word 2007

No matter how experienced you are, there will always be times when you need help to find out how to do something in Word 2007. It is a very large and powerful program with a multitude of features. There are several ways to get help, but don't look for the Office Assistant, as it has now been switched off for good!

The Built-in Microsoft Help System

All of the Office 2007 applications operate in the same way. If you press the **F1** function key, or click the **Help** toolbar button shown here, the Help window will open as shown in Fig. 1.15 below.

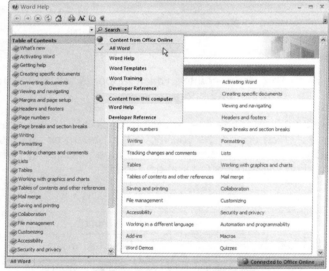

Fig. 1.15 The Microsoft Office Help Window

The program expects you to be 'Online', or connected to the Internet. In fact, if you are not, it will attempt to connect you. You can control where Help searches for its content in two ways. If you click the down arrow to the right of the **Search** button a drop-down menu opens as shown in Fig. 1.15. This has several online and PC based options. If you click the **Word Help** option under **Content from this computer** the Help system will only look on your computer for its help data.

Fig. 1.16 Connection Status Menu

Whether you are looking at **Help** online or offline is shown in the lower-right corner of the Help window, as shown in Fig. 1.15.

Clicking this area with the mouse opens the **Connection Status** menu shown in Fig. 1.16. As can be seen, this offers an easier way to tell **Help** where to look for its content. This setting is retained after you close the Help window, so if you don't want to search online you only have to set this once.

In the Help window the **Table of Contents** list opens up a list of available help topics in the form of closed books. Left-clicking one of these books opens it and displays a further list of topics with an icon, as shown in Fig. 1.17.

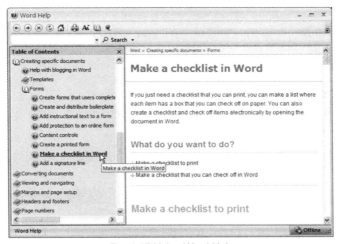

Fig. 1.17 Using Word Help

Clicking any of these opens the relevant Help page in the right-hand pane as shown in Fig 1.17. We suggest you try looking up 'what's new' – it is an excellent starting point in learning how to use the Office Help System.

If you want to know more about the options in a dialogue box, click the **Help** button ? in the top right corner of the box. This will open the Help window usually with relevant help showing in the right-hand pane.

Searching Help

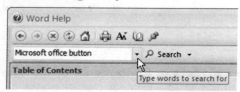

Fig. 1.18 Typing Words to Search For

A quick way to find what you want in the Help system is to enter the text you want to search for in the **Type words to search for** box, as shown here in Fig. 1.18. A search using 2 to 7 words returns the most accurate results. If you want to repeat a search, you click the down arrow to the right of the **Type words to search for** list, and then click the search term that you want in the list.

The Help Toolbar

You can control the Help window with the buttons on the toolbar, as follows:

Back – Opens the last Help page viewed in the current session list.

Forward – Opens the previous Help page viewed in the current session list.

Stop – Stops loading a document.

Refresh – Re-loads the current Help page.

Home – Opens the first (or Home) Help page for the open application.

 Print – Opens the Print dialogue box to let you print all, or a selection, of the current Help topic.

 Change Font Size – Opens a sub-menu to let you control the size of text in the Help window.

 Hide/Show Table of Contents – A toggle key which closes or reopens the left pane of the Help window, giving more room for the Help text.

 Keep On Top/Not On Top – A toggle key you can click to keep the Help window displaying on top of, or below, any open Office 2007 applications.

The Help system is quite comprehensive and it is usually easy to find the information you are looking for. We strongly recommend that you spend some time here to learn about the programs. An hour now may well save many hours later!

Screen Tips

If you want to know what a particular button or feature does you can also get Screen Tips help. For information on a particular button or feature, rest the pointer on it and a floating box will appear as shown in Fig. 1.19 below.

Fig. 1.19 A Typical Screen Tip Floating Box

Here we hovered the pointer over the **Change Case** button and a quite detailed description was given. This feature is much improved in Office 2007 applications.

Word 2007 File Formats

With version 2007, Word now uses the Microsoft Office Open XML file formats, based on Extensible Markup Language (XML). File extensions change from .doc to .docx. If you are saving a file with macros, the extension changes again to .docxm, so you know if the file contains macros or not.

XML files have practical advantages. Each file is actually a zip file of individual elements. If your file gets corrupted, it's easier to recover more of the data. They are compressed to around half the size of earlier Word files.

We list below all the default file extensions for Word 2007.

XML file type Extension Document	.docx
Macro-enabled document	.docm
Template	.dotx
Macro-enabled template	.dotm

If you need to, you can still save your files in the older formats with the **Save As** command, but all the .XML advantages will be lost.

Word 2007 can open files created in all previous versions of Word in 'compatibility' mode. You know this because at the top of the document "(Compatibility Mode)" appears next to the name of the file. You can then convert the older document to the new file format by clicking the **Office Button**, then the **Convert** command on the drop-down menu.

The new file format also gives you the ability to use features that are available only in Office 2007. One example of such a feature is the new SmartArt Graphics. The new file format supports plenty of other new features, such as math equations, themes, and content controls.

To open Word 2007 files with earlier versions of Word, you need to install the **Microsoft Office Compatibility Pack for 2007 Office Word, Excel and PowerPoint File Formats** as well as any necessary Office updates. Using this Compatibility Pack, you can open, edit some items, and save Word 2007 documents in previous Office versions. Just go to the Microsoft Download Center to find the pack.

2

The New User Interface

Pick and Click

When you open Word 2007 you will notice that the program interface has changed quite dramatically. The menu and toolbar design of previous versions has been replaced with a new user interface to make it easier to find and use all the available commands and features. 'Pick and Click' is very much the order of the day. This is somewhat daunting at first, but once you start using the new interface you will very rapidly get used to it.

The Ribbon

Traditional menus and toolbars have been replaced by the Ribbon – a new device that presents commands organised into a set of tabs, as shown in Fig.2.1 below.

Fig. 2.1 The Home Tab of the Word 2007 Ribbon

The tabs on the Ribbon display the commands that are most relevant for each of the task areas in an application, as shown here for Word 2007. There are four basic components to the Ribbon.

Tabs   There are seven basic tabs across the top, each representing an activity area.

Groups   Each tab has several groups that show related items together.

Commands Buttons that you click to action.

Dialogue Box Launcher – Many groups have an arrow icon in the lower-right corner to open an 'old style' dialogue box.

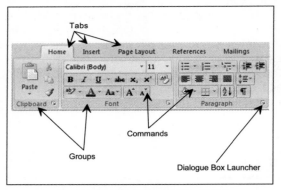

Fig. 2.2 The Components of a Ribbon

The Home tab contains all the things you use most often, such as the **Cut** and **Paste** commands and those used for formatting, and for changing text font, size, bold, italic, and so on. Clicking a new tab opens a new series of groups, each with its relevant command buttons. This really works very well.

The Ribbon is scalable, and adapts to different sized screens or windows. It displays smaller versions of tabs and groups as screen resolution decreases. When you make the Ribbon smaller, the groups on the open tab begin to shrink horizontally. The most commonly used commands or features are left open as the program window shrinks. Word 2007 is probably best used with large high resolution screens, but there again, so is almost everything else in computing!

Dialogue Box Launcher

The new Ribbons hold the most commonly used command buttons for the program, but by no means all of the available commands. Some groups have a small diagonal arrow in the lower-right corner.

 This is the new **Dialogue Box Launcher**. You click it to see more options related to that group. They often appear as a Dialogue box similar to those of previous versions of Word, as shown in Fig. 2.3 below.

Fig. 2.3 The Font Dialogue Box (Vista)

This was opened by clicking the **Dialogue Box Launcher** located on the **Font** group of the **Home** tab of the Word 2007 Ribbon.

To confuse matters slightly, some **Dialogue Box Launchers** actually open task panes, not dialogue boxes. Try clicking the Launcher on the **Home**, **Clipboard** group, to see what we mean.

Contextual Tabs

Not all of the available tabs are visible. Some only appear when they are needed.

As an example, clicking on a picture in a document opens a contextual tab on the Ribbon with commands used for editing the picture, as shown in Fig. 2.4 below. Once you leave the picture, by clicking outside it, this **Picture Tools** tab disappears. Very clever.

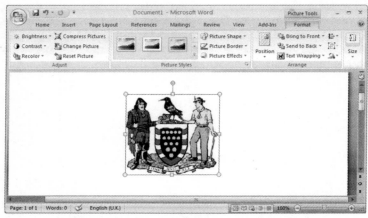

Fig. 2.4 Word 2007's Contextual Picture Tools Tab

Hiding the Ribbon

The Ribbon makes everything in Word 2007 centralised and easy to find, but there are times when you just want to work on your document.

You can maximise your working area by hiding the Ribbon. To do this just double-click the active tab. All the groups just disappear. Go on, try it. When you want to see the commands again, double-click the active tab to bring back the groups.

If you find you hate the Ribbon in Word 2007 you have a problem as there is no direct way to delete or replace it with the toolbars and menus from the earlier versions. If you are really desperate you could, however, try the add-in mentioned on page 3. Not having tried this ourselves, we can't recommend it, but it looks to be one solution.

Ribbon Keyboard Shortcuts

Those of you who have trouble using a mouse will be glad to hear that all the Ribbon features are available from the keyboard using what are now called **Key Tips**.

Pressing the **Alt** key makes Key Tip badges appear for all Ribbon tabs, the Quick Access Toolbar commands, and the Microsoft Office Button, as shown in Fig. 2.5 below.

Fig. 2.5 Word 2007 Ribbon Showing Key Tips

Then you can press the Key Tip for the tab you want to display. If that tab is the active one, all the Key Tips for the tab's commands appear, as we show in Fig. 2.6 below, where we pressed the 'H' keyboard key. Then you can press the Key Tip for the command you want.

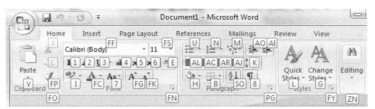

Fig. 2.6 Word's Home Tab Key Tips

When you press a Key Tip for a non-active tab, the tab is opened and all the Key Tips for the tab's commands appear.

Access keys let you quickly use commands by pressing a few keystrokes, no matter where you are in the program. To close them you press the **Alt** key again.

You can still use the old **Alt+** shortcuts that accessed menus and commands in previous versions of Office applications, but because the old menus are no longer available you need to know the full shortcuts to use them.

Shortcuts that start with the **Ctrl** key, such as **Ctrl+C** for copy, remain the same as in previous versions.

The Microsoft Office Button

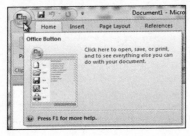

Fig. 2.7 The Office Button Screen Tip

The **Office Button** is in the upper-left corner of most Office 2007 program windows. It replaces the File menu of previous versions, lists recently opened documents, and gives access to the application's control options, as shown in Fig. 2.8.

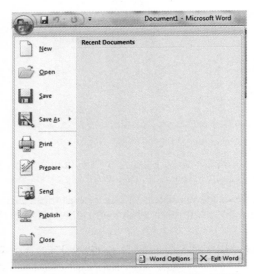

Fig. 2.8 The Office Button Menu for Word 2007

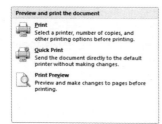

Fig. 2.9 The Print Sub-Menu

You click the **Office Button** to: **Open** a new or existing document, **Save** the current one in a range of file formats, **Save As** another name or format, **Send** it as an e-mail, or **Print** the current document, as well as a range of new commands such as **Prepare**, **Send** and **Publish**.

Clicking the **Print** button opens a sub-menu, as shown above, giving easy access to your printer controls.

To change an application's settings in previous Office versions you clicked **Options** on the **Tools** menu. Now, all these settings are part of Word Options, which you open by clicking the **Options** button on the bottom of the Office Button menu. In Fig. 2.8 on the previous page, you would click the **Word Options** button to open the Word Options box, shown in Fig. 2.10 below.

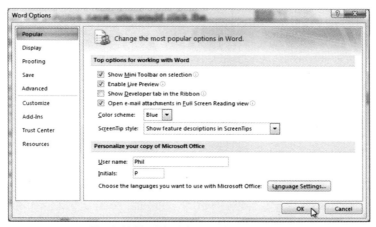

Fig. 2.10 The Word Options Dialogue Box

This dialogue box lets you change any of Word's settings and defaults.

The Mini Toolbar

Some commands are so useful that you want to have them immediately available whatever you are doing. For these, Word 2007 shows a 'hovering' Mini Toolbar over your work when they are available.

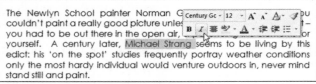

The Newlyn School painter Norman G couldn't paint a really good picture unles you had to be out there in the open air, yourself. A century later, Michael Strang seems to be living by this edict: his 'on the spot' studies frequently portray weather conditions only the most hardy individual would venture outdoors in, never mind stand still and paint.

Fig. 2.11 A Mini Toolbar of Word Formatting Commands

In the example above, we were working on the Page Layout tab of Word 2007 and wanted to quickly format some text. We selected it by dragging the mouse pointer and then pointed at the selection. A faded Mini toolbar appeared, which when pointed to became solid, as shown in Fig. 2.11. This offered a range of formatting options without having to go to any of the tabs on the Ribbon.

A Mini Toolbar will stay active for a selection until you click the document outside the selection. It will then disappear.

Galleries

Galleries are at the heart of the redesigned 'Pick and Click' interface. They provide you with a set of clear visual results to choose from when you are working in a document.

By presenting a simple set of potential results, rather than a complex dialogue box with numerous options, Galleries simplify the process of producing good-looking work. As we have seen, dialogue boxes are still available if you want more control over an operation, but a simple Gallery choice will very often be enough.

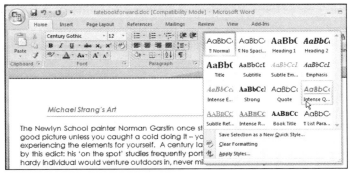

Fig. 2.12 A Style Gallery in Word 2007

As we show above, you can apply pre-set formats and styles from galleries in the Ribbon. In Fig. 2.12 the result of applying the style is shown in the Gallery.

Live Preview

Live Preview is a new feature to Word 2007. It previews the results of applying an editing or formatting change as you move the pointer over the options in a Gallery.

In our example above, as we moved the pointer over the style options in the gallery, the document heading automatically changed to show how it would look if that style were chosen.

Live previews work for borders, fills, rotation, bullets and numbering, outline styles, fine-tuning pictures, textures and styles.

Quick Access Toolbar

The Quick Access Toolbar is the small area to the upper left of the Ribbon, as shown in Fig. 1.1 on page 2. It contains buttons for the things that you use over and over every day, such as **Save**, **Undo**, and **Repeat**, by default. The bar is always available, whatever you are doing in a program.

Fig. 2.13 The Quick
Access Toolbar

It is very easy to add your favourite commands to the Quick Access toolbar so they are available no matter which tab you are on. Here in Fig. 2.13 we have added a **Print Preview** command button. To do this we clicked the **Customize Quick Access Toolbar** button ⊟ and selected **More Commands** from the drop-down menu. This opened the Word Options box as shown in Fig. 2.14.

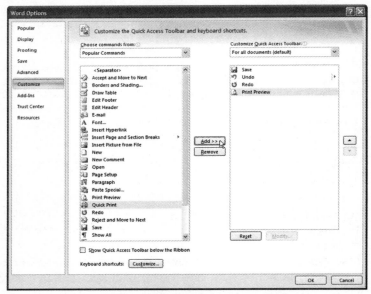

Fig. 2.14 Customising the Quick Access Toolbar

In the Customize tab, shown open above, you select any commands in the left pane and click the **Add** button to place them on the Quick Access toolbar. To remove them just do the opposite. You can control where the new button displays by selecting them in the right pane and clicking the up and down arrows on the right-hand side. When you are happy click the **OK** button.

3

Microsoft Word 2007 Basics

Fig. 3.1 Word's Flash Screen

Microsoft's Word 2007, part of the Office 2007 package, is without doubt the best Windows word processor so far. As you would expect, it is fully integrated with all the other Office 2007 applications. You will find using the redesigned Word 2007 program to be even more intuitive and easy than earlier versions and you will soon be producing the type of word processed output you would not have dreamt possible.

The new Ribbon in Word 2007 groups tools by task, and the commands you use most frequently are close at hand. This new, results-oriented interface presents tools to you, in a clear and organised fashion, when you need them. You now get a live visual preview of the formatting in your document before you actually make a change.

New chart and diagram features include three-dimensional shapes, transparency, drop shadows, and other effects. Quick Styles and Document Themes, let you quickly change the appearance of text, tables, and graphics throughout your document.

In many situations Word 2007 will attempt to anticipate what you want to do and will probably produce the correct result most of the time. For example, AutoCorrect and AutoFormat can, when active, correct common spelling mistakes and format documents automatically.

Starting the Word Program

To start Word 2007, use the ***start***, **All Programs** command, select the **Microsoft Office** entry from the menu, and click **Microsoft Office Word 2007** as shown for XP in Fig. 3.2.

Fig. 3.2 Using the Start Menu

You can also double-click on a Word document file in a Windows folder, in which case the document will be loaded into Word at the same time.

When you start Word the program momentarily displays its opening flash screen, (Fig. 3.1), and then displays the first page of a new document, shown in Fig. 3.3 below. We will come back to this window shortly.

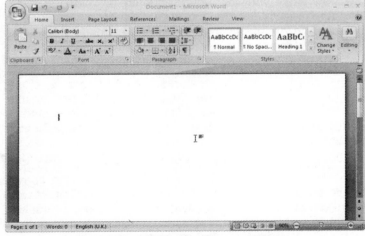

Fig. 3.3 Word 2007's New Document Window

Whether you have used a previous version of Word or not, the first time you use the program, it might be a good idea to click the **Microsoft Office Word Help** button on the Ribbon, or press the **F1** keyboard key. These open the Word Help window shown in Fig. 3.4 below.

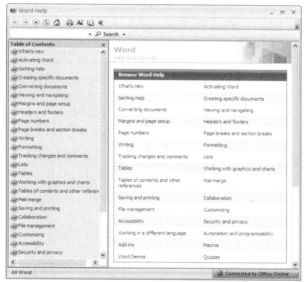

Fig. 3.4 The Word Help System

In the Help window the **Table of Contents** list opens up a list of available help topics in the form of closed books . Left-clicking one of these books opens it and displays a further list of topics with icons. Clicking any of these opens the relevant Help page in the right-hand pane.

We suggest you try looking up 'What's new' – it is an excellent starting point in learning how to use the Word 2007 program. After looking at this, have a look at the other options in the **Table of Contents** list.

We suggest you spend a little time here browsing through the various topics before going on. It should be time well spent. You may well also want to read our section starting on page 16 about the Help system itself.

The Word Screen

The opening 'blank' screen of Word 2007 is shown below. It is perhaps worth spending some time looking at the various parts that make up this screen. Word follows the usual Windows and Office 2007 conventions and if you are familiar with these you can skip some of this section, but even so, a few minutes might be well spent here.

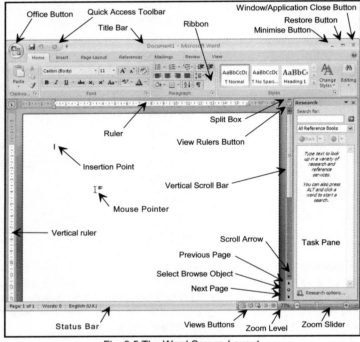

Fig. 3.5 The Word Screen Layout

The Task Pane shown open above only appears during certain operations, so don't spend too long looking for it. The layout, as shown, is in a window, but if you click on the application **Restore** button, you can make Word take up the full screen area available. Using a window can be useful when you are running several applications at the same time and you want to transfer between them with the mouse.

The Word 2007 window is divided into several areas which have the following functions:

Area	*Function*
Office Button	Located in the upper-left corner of the program window. This button replaces the File menu of previous versions, lists recently opened documents, and gives access to the application's control options.
Quick Access Toolbar	Located to the right of the Office button, it contains buttons that are always available for your most common commands, such as Save, Undo, and Repeat, by default.
Title Bar	The bar at the top of a window which displays the application name and the name of the current document.
Minimise Button	When clicked on, this button minimises the application to an icon on the Windows Taskbar.
Restore Button	When clicked on, this button restores the active window to the position and size that was occupied before it was maximised.
	The restore button is then replaced by a Maximise button, as shown here, which is used to set the window to full screen size.
Close button	The extreme top right button that you click to close a window.

Ribbon	Traditional menus and toolbars have been replaced by the Ribbon, a new device that presents commands organised into a set of tabs. Each tab has several Groups that show related Command items together.
Gallery	A control that displays a choice visually so that you can see the results that you will get.
Rulers	The horizontal and vertical bars where you can see and set page margins, tabulation points and indents.
Split Box	The ▬ box at the top of the vertical scroll bar which when dragged allows you to split the screen.
View Rulers Button	The toggle button 🔲 below the Split Box that you click to turn the rulers on and off.
Scroll Bars	The areas on the screen that contain scroll boxes in vertical and horizontal bars. Clicking on these bars allows you to control the part of a document which is visible on the screen.
Scroll Arrows	The arrowheads at each end of each scroll bar which you can click to scroll the screen up and down one line, or left and right 10% of the screen, at a time.
Insertion Point	The pointer used to indicate where text will be inserted.
Views Buttons	Clicking these buttons changes screen views quickly.

Status Bar   The bottom line of a document's window that displays status information.

Zoom Slider   The slider to the right of the Status Bar that controls the zoom level.

Note that in Fig. 3.5, the Word window displays an empty document with the title 'Document1', and has a solid 'Title bar', indicating that it is the active application window. Although multiple windows can be displayed simultaneously, you can only enter data into the active window (which will always be displayed on top, unless you view them on a split screen). Title bars of non-active windows appear a lighter shade than that of the active one.

The Ribbon

When you first use Word 2007 the Ribbon is the first major change you will notice. Microsoft have spent many thousands of 'man hours' designing a new intuitive user interface. The older menu bar and toolbars have been scrapped and replaced with the Ribbon. Please look at page 21 for a general description of the main Ribbon components.

In Word the Ribbon has seven tabs, each one with the most used controls grouped on it for the main program actions.

Fig. 3.6 The Home Tab of the Word 2007 Ribbon

A quick look at the Home tab, shown in Fig. 3.6, shows that it contains all the things you use most often, such as the cut and paste commands and those used for formatting both text, paragraphs and styles, such as changing text font, size, bold, italic, and so on. Clicking a new tab opens a new series of groups, each with its relevant command buttons, as shown in the next series of figures.

Fig. 3.7 The Insert Tab of the Word 2007 Ribbon

Under the Insert tab, are groupings to enable you to immediately insert Pages, Tables, Illustrations, Links, Headers and Footers, Text, and Symbols.

Fig. 3.8 The Page Layout Tab of the Word 2007 Ribbon

The Page Layout tab groups controls for you to set your Themes, Page Setup, Page Background, Paragraph and to Arrange graphic content.

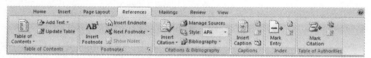

Fig. 3.9 The References Tab of the Word 2007 Ribbon

You will use the References tab most with large documents and reports, to add and control a Table of Contents, Footnotes, Citations and Bibliography, Captions, an Index and a Table of Authorities.

Fig. 3.10 The Mailings Tab of the Word 2007 Ribbon

The Mailings tab groups all the actions involved in sending your personal and office correspondence. These include Creating envelopes and labels, Starting a Mail Merge, Writing and Inserting Fields to control a mail merge, letting you Preview Results and then Finish a merge operation.

Fig. 3.11 The Review Tab of the Word 2007 Ribbon

The Review tab groups controls for Proofing your documents and to initiate and track document review and approval processes in an organisation for instance. It lets you handle Comments, document Tracking, any Changes made to a document and lets you Compare or Protect your documents.

Fig. 3.12 The View Tab of the Word 2007 Ribbon

The View tab is where you go to set what you see on the screen. You can choose between Document Views, Show or Hide screen features, Zoom to different magnifications, control document Windows and run and record Macros.

That is all the fixed Tabs looked at, but there are still others, as described on page 23. Some Tabs only appear when they are actually needed. These contextual tabs contain tools that are only active when an object like a picture, chart or equation is selected in the document. These will be covered later, as and when they crop up.

Quick Access Toolbar

The Quick Access Toolbar is the small area to the upper left of the Ribbon, as shown in Fig. 3.13. This is one of the most useful new features of Word 2007. It contains buttons for the things that you use over and over every day, such as **Save**, **Undo**, and **Repeat**, by default. The bar is always available, whatever you are doing in a program, and it is very easy to add buttons for your most used commands.

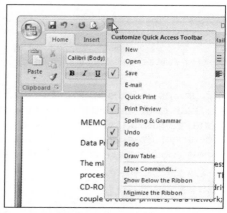

Fig. 3.13 Customising the Quick Access Toolbar

Clicking the **Customize Quick Access Toolbar** button pointed to above shows a menu of suggested items for the toolbar. You can select the **More Commands** option to add others (see page 30), or even easier, just right-click on a Ribbon control and select **Add to Quick Access Toolbar**.

 The buttons at the bottom right of the document area of Fig. 3.5, shown enlarged here, can be used to go to the **Previous Page**, to **Select Browse Object**, or go to the **Next Page**. Clicking the **Select Browse Object** button, in the middle of the three, reveals a list of objects, as shown in Fig. 3.14, that you can use to browse your document.

Fig. 3.14 Selecting Objects to Browse

For example, you can browse by Page (going from one page to the next, by Section (going from one section to the next), or by Picture going from one picture to the next), to mention but a few.

To see which option is which, place the mouse pointer on an object and its function will replace the **Cancel** button.

The Status Bar

This is located at the bottom of the Word window and is used to display statistics about the active document.

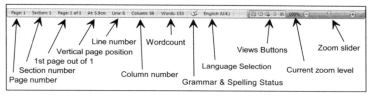

Fig. 3.15 The Word 2007 Status Bar

For example, when a document is being opened, the **Status Bar** displays for a short time its name and length in terms of total number of characters. Once a document is opened, the **Status Bar** displays the statistics of the document at the insertion point; here it is on Page 1, Section 1, and 56 characters from the left margin.

You can control what appears on the **Status Bar** by right-clicking it and making selections in the Customize Status Box that opens.

Fig. 3.16 The Find and Replace Box

Double-clicking on the left items of the **Status Bar** displays the Find and Replace dialogue box, as shown in Fig. 3.16. This is shown with the **Go To** tab selected. You can choose which page, section line, etc., of the document to go to, or you can use the other tabs to **Find** and **Replace** text (more about this later). Double-clicking many of the other items on the **Status Bar** will also activate their features.

Creating Word Documents

When the program is first used, all Word's features default to those shown in Fig. 3.3. It is quite possible to use Word in this mode, without changing any main settings, but obviously it is possible to customise the package to your needs, as we shall see later.

Entering Text

In order to illustrate some of Word's capabilities, you need to have a short text at hand. We suggest you type the memo below into a new document. At this stage, don't worry if the length of the lines below differ from those on your display.

As you type in text, any time you want to force a new line, or paragraph, just press the **Enter** key. While typing within a paragraph, Word sorts out line lengths automatically (known as 'word wrap'), without you having to press any keys to move to a new line.

MEMO TO PC USERS

Data Processing Computers

The microcomputers in the Data Processing room are a mixture of IBM compatible PCs with Pentium processors running at various speeds. They all have 3.5" floppy drives of 1.44MB capacity, some with CD-ROM drives, and some with DVD drives. The PCs are connected to various printers, including a couple of colour printers, via a network; the Laser printers giving best output.

The computer you are using will have at least a 300 GB capacity hard disc on which a number of software programs, including the latest version of Microsoft Windows and Microsoft Office, have been installed. To make life easier, the hard disc is partitioned so that data can be kept separate from programs. The disc partition that holds the data for the various applications running on the computer is highly structured, with each program having its own folder in which its own data can be held.

Fig. 3.17 A Short Memo to Illustrate some of Word's Capabilities

Moving Around a Document

You can move the cursor around a document with the normal direction keys, and with the key combinations listed below.

To move	Press
Left one character	←
Right one character	→
Up one line	↑
Down one line	↓
Left one word	Ctrl+←
Right one word	Ctrl+→
To beginning of line	Home
To end of line	End
To paragraph beginning	Ctrl+↑
To paragraph end	Ctrl+↓
Up one screen	PgUp
Down one screen	PgDn
To top of previous page	Ctrl+PgUp
To top of next page	Ctrl+PgDn
To beginning of file	Ctrl+Home
To end of file	Ctrl+End

Fig. 3.18 The Vertical Scroll Bar

To move to a specified page in a multi-page document, either drag the vertical scroll bar up or down until the required page number is shown, as in Fig. 3.18, or use the **Ctrl+G** keyboard shortcut, or **Go To** as described on page 41. This can also be actioned from the **Editing** group on the Home tab.

To easily step from page to page you can also click the **Previous Page** ✱ and **Next Page** ✱ buttons, also shown in Fig. 3.18.

Obviously, you need to become familiar with these methods of moving around a document, particularly if you spot an error in a document which needs to be corrected, which is the subject of the latter half of this chapter.

Themes, Templates and Styles

Fig. 3.19 The Styles Gallery on the Home Tab

When you start Word it opens with a new empty document, and defaults to the 'Normal' style in the Styles gallery as shown in Fig. 3.19. This means that any text you enter is shown in the Normal style which is one of the styles available in the NORMAL template. Every document produced by Word has to use a template, and NORMAL is the default. A template is a special "starter" document type. When you open a template, a new document opens with the content, layout, formatting, styles, and the theme from that template.

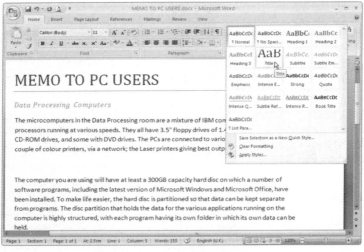

Fig. 3.20 Using the Styles Gallery

To change the style of a paragraph, place the cursor in the paragraph in question, the title line in our example, and move the pointer through the options in the Style gallery. Each one is instantly previewed in the main body of the document. We clicked on the **Title** style to select it and the paragraph reformatted to Cambria typeface of point size 26 with a line across the page. Very clever.

Fig. 3.21 The
Styles Task Pane

Another way of setting a style is from the floating Styles Task Pane which is opened by clicking the **Dialogue Box Launcher** on the **Styles** group of the **Home** tab, as pointed to here in Fig. 3.21.

Now with the cursor in the second line of text, we selected *Subtitle* which reformatted the line of text to Cambria 12, blue italic. Your memo should now look presentable, and be similar to Fig. 3.20 on the facing page.

If you try both methods you may find that in the long run the Styles Task Pane, or window, method is better. You can carry out most, if not all, of your style format work from the Task Pane. But of course you will use which method you prefer. Possibly the Styles gallery for simple reformatting and the Task Pane for more complicated work.

You have probably noticed that the body of the memo is in Calibri typeface of point size 11, the new Office 2007 default for the **Normal** style. Later on we will discuss how to also change this font.

Themes

Fig. 3.22 The
Themes Group

Every document you create in Office 2007 now has a Theme inside it. Themes do not contain text or data, but colours, fonts, or effects that apply to all parts of the document. Themes simplify the process of creating matching, documents across all the Office 2007 programs.

To try different themes, rest your pointer over a thumbnail in the Themes gallery, on the Page Layout tab, and notice how your document changes.

Document Screen Views

Fig. 3.23 Document
Views Group

Word 2007 provides five main display views, **Print Layout**, **Full Screen Reading, Web Layout**, **Outline** and **Draft**, as well as **Document Map** and **Thumbnails** views. You can also view your documents in a whole range of screen enlargements with the **Zoom** controls. You control these viewing options, either from the **Status Bar**, or from the **View** tab of the Ribbon. The **Document Views** group is shown in Fig. 3.23. When a document is displayed you can switch freely between them. When first loaded, the screen displays in the default **Print Layout** view.

The main view options have the following effect, and can also be accessed by clicking the **Views** buttons on the **Status Bar** at the bottom of the Word window (see Fig. 3.5).

Draft

A view that simplifies the layout of the page so that you can type, edit and format text quickly. In draft view, page boundaries, headers and footers, backgrounds, drawing objects, and pictures that do not have the **'In line with text'** wrapping style do not appear.

Web Layout

A view that optimises the layout of a document to make online reading easier. Use this layout view when you are creating a Web page or a document that is viewed on the screen. In Web layout view, you can see backgrounds, text is wrapped to fit the window, and graphics are positioned just as they are in a Web browser.

Print Layout

Provides a WYSIWYG (what you see is what you get) view of a document. The text displays in the typefaces and point sizes and with the selected attributes.

This is the usual working view and all document features appear on the screen as they will in the final printout.

Full Screen Reading

Provides an easy to read and very customisable view of a document. You can change the text size, edit the document, carry out commenting and reviews and see how the pages will print. Also in this view you have easy access to research, translation and highlighting tools.

Outline

Provides a collapsible view of a document, which enables you to see its organisation at a glance. You can display all the text in a file, or just the text that uses the paragraph styles you specify.

Document Map

This view displays a separate pane with a list of document headings. You can quickly navigate through the document, when you click a heading Word jumps to that place in the document and displays the heading at the top of the window.

Thumbnails

This view displays a pane on the left with a small image, or thumbnail, of each page of the document. You can quickly navigate through the document by clicking the thumbnails.

Changing Word's Default Options

Modifying Margins

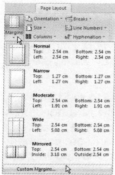

It is easy to change the standard page margins for your entire document from the cursor position onward, or for selected text (more about this later).

Click the **Page Layout**, **Page Setup**, **Margins** button on the Ribbon, as shown in Fig. 3.24. There is a gallery of five preset options to select from, or you can click the **Custom Margins** option to open the Page Setup dialogue box shown in Fig. 3.25 below. On the margins tab of this box you can change any of the margin or gutter settings.

Fig. 3.24 Changing Margin Settings

Fig. 3.25 The Margins Tab Sheet of the Page Setup Box

The **Preview** diagram at the bottom of the box shows how your changes will look on a real page. The orientation of the printed page is normally **Portrait** where text prints across the page width, but you can change this to **Landscape** which prints across the page length, if you prefer.

To make the new settings 'permanent', press the **Default** button and confirm that you wish this change to affect all new documents based on the Normal template.

Changing Paper Settings

To change the default paper settings from those set during installation you do the following.

As before open the Page Setup box, but click the Paper tab. Click the down-arrow against the **Paper size** box to reveal the list of available paper sizes, as shown in Fig. 3.26. Change the page size to your new choice, probably A4.

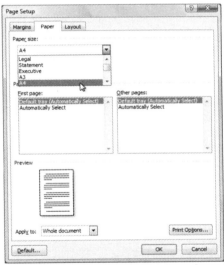

Fig. 3.26 The Paper Tab Sheet of the Page Setup Box

Any changes you can make to your document from the Page Setup dialogue box can be applied to either the whole document or to the rest of the document starting from the current position of the insertion pointer. To set this, click the down-arrow button against the **Apply to** box and choose from the drop-down list. As before, click the **Default** button to make your changes affect all your new documents.

The **Paper source** section of the Page Setup box lets you set where your printer takes its paper from. You might have a printer that holds paper in trays, in which case you might want to specify that the **First page** (headed paper perhaps), should be taken from one tray, while **Other pages** should be taken from a different tray.

Modifying the Page Layout

Clicking the Layout tab of the Page Setup box, displays the following sheet, from which you can set options for headers and footers, section breaks, vertical alignment and whether to add line numbers or borders.

Fig. 3.27 The Layout Tab Sheet of the Page Setup Box

The default for **Section Start** is 'New Page' which allows the section to start at the top of the next page. Pressing the down arrow against this option, allows you to change this.

In the Headers and Footers section of the dialogue box, you can specify whether you want one header or footer for even-numbered pages and a different header or footer for odd-numbered pages. You can further specify if you want a different header or footer on the first page from the header or footer used for the rest of the document. Word aligns the top line with the 'Top' margin, but this can be changed with the **Vertical alignment** option.

Changing Other Default Options

You can also change the other default options available to you in Word 2007, by clicking the **Office Button** (see page 26) and selecting the **Word Options** command. This opens the Word Options dialogue box shown in Fig. 3.28.

Fig. 3.28 The Word Options Dialogue Box

As can be seen, this box has nine tabbed sheets which give you control of most of the program's settings. A few minutes spent here will help you understand the workings of Word 2007.

Saving to a File

The quickest way to save a document to disc is to click the **Save** button on the Quick Access toolbar. The usual way however is from the **Office Button** menu, shown in Fig. 3.29 below, which gives you more control of the saving operation.

Fig. 3.29 Saving Operations from the Office Button

- **Save** is used when a document has previously been saved to disc in a named file; using this command saves your work under the existing filename automatically without prompting you.

- **Save As** (selected above) is used when you want to save your document with a different name or file format, or in a different location.

Using the **Save As** command (or the first time you use the **Save** command when a document has no name), opens the dialogue box shown in Fig. 3.30 (for Windows XP).

Note that the first 255 characters of the first paragraph of a new document are placed and highlighted in the **File name** field box, with the program waiting for you to over-type a new name.

Filenames must have less than 255 characters and cannot include any of the following keyboard characters: /, \, >, <, *, ?, ", |, :, or ;. Word 2007 adds the new file extension **.docx** automatically and uses it to identify its documents.

Fig. 3.30 The File Save As Box

You can select a drive other than the one displayed, by clicking the down arrow against the **Save in** text box. You can also select a folder in which to save your work. The large buttons on the left of the box give rapid access to six possible saving locations. To create a new folder use the **Create New Folder** button, as shown pointed to below.

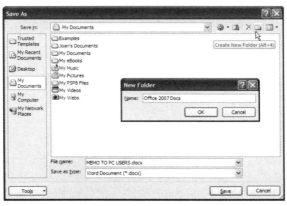

Fig. 3.31 Creating a New Folder

We used this facility to create a folder called **Office 2007 Docs** within the **My Documents** folder (**Documents** folder in Windows Vista). To save our work currently in memory, we selected this folder in the **Save in** field of the Save As dialogue box, then moved the cursor into the **File name** box, and typed **PC User1**. We suggest you do the same. The name currently displayed in the box is the title of our memo which Word offers as a suitable filename.

By clicking the **Save as type** button at the bottom of the Save As dialogue box, you can save the Document Template, or the Text Only parts of your work, or you can save your document in a variety of 26 formats, including Rich Text, and several Web Page options. The default is always **.docx**, the Word 2007 document file type.

Fig. 3.32 Saving a Document as a Different Type

With Windows Vista the procedures are very similar, but the dialogue boxes have been re-designed, as in Fig. 3.33.

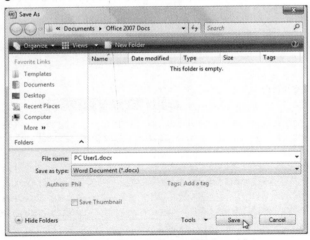

Fig. 3.33 The Save As Box in Windows Vista

Vista Folder Features

In Vista, most folders and file related dialogue boxes have the following features.

Back and Forward buttons ◉◉▾ – Used to navigate to other folders you have already opened.

Address bar `◌ ▸ Computer ▸ OS (C:) ▸ Users ▸ Phil ▸    ▾ ↻` – Used to navigate to a different folder without closing the current folder window.

Search box `Search     ⌕` – Type a word or phrase in this, to look for a file or sub-folder stored in the current folder.

Toolbar `◌ Organize ▾  ▤ Views ▾  ◌ New Folder` – Click buttons to perform common tasks, such as organising your files and folders, setting different views of them and creating a new folder. The toolbar buttons depend on the action you are carrying out.

Navigation pane – Lets you change the view to other folders. The Favorite links section makes it easy to change to a common folder.

File list – This shows the contents of the current folder.

Tags – Depending on the type of file you are saving, you might be able to add file properties (like author or key words) to act as tags. Later, you can search and organise files using these property tags.

Selecting File Location

You can select where Word automatically looks for your document files when you first choose to open or save a document, by clicking the **Office Button** ◉, selecting the **Word Options** command and clicking the Save tab of the displayed Word Options dialogue box, (Fig. 3.34 on the next page), and modifying the location of the **Default file location**. Our **Default file location** is given as C:\Users\Phil\Documents\ which with our Vista setup is the **Documents** folder.

Microsoft suggests that you store documents, worksheets, presentations, databases, and other files you are currently working on, in the **Documents** folder (Vista), or in **My Documents** (Windows XP). These are easily accessed from the Desktop with the **Start** menu. This, of course, is a matter of preference, so we leave it to you to decide. We prefer to create sub-folders within **Documents** to group our files in.

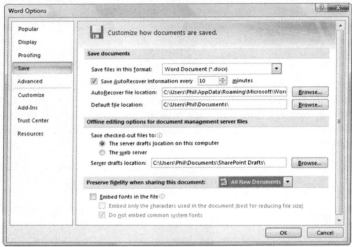

Fig. 3.34 Setting Word's File Locations

While any of the file opening, saving and location dialogue boxes are open you can use them to generally manage your files and folders. You do this by right-clicking on the name of a file or folder you want to manipulate. A context sensitive menu is opened like ours in Fig. 3.35.

Fig. 3.35 A Context Menu

All of these options may not be available on your system, but the common ones of Open, New, Print, Cut, Copy, Create Shortcut, Delete, Rename and Properties should always be there.

Closing a Document

There are several ways to close a document in Word. Once you have saved it you can click its window close ▆▆ button. If you only have one document open in Word this will close the program, in which case it is better to click the **Office Button** 🗐 and use the **Close** command, shown in Fig. 3.29.

If the document (or file) has changed since the last time it was saved, you will be given the option to save it before it is removed from memory.

If a document is not closed before a new document is opened, then both documents will be held in memory in their own Word windows, but only one will be the current

Fig. 3.36 Open Documents

document. To find out which documents are held in memory, look at the Windows Taskbar at the bottom of the screen (but see the section below), or click the **Switch Windows** command on the View tab of the Ribbon to see a list as shown in Fig. 3.36.

In this case, the first document in the list is the current one, and to make another document current, just click it in the list.

To close a document which is not the current one, use the **Switch Windows** command to make it current, and close it with one of the above methods.

Note – With Word 2007 it is possible to limit what is shown on the Taskbar. By default all your open Word documents will each have an entry on the Taskbar. But you can change this so that only the current, or active, document is shown there.

Fig. 3.37 Some Word Options

To do this, click the **Office Button** 🗐 and select the **Word Options** command. This opens the Word Options dialogue box shown in

Fig. 3.28. Open the Advanced tab sheet and in the **Display** section, uncheck the **Show all windows in taskbar** option, as shown here. To return to the default Taskbar display, just click in the check box again.

Opening a Document

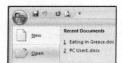

Fig. 3.38 Part of
Office Button Menu

You can use the Open dialogue box in Word, shown in Fig. 3.39 below, to open documents that might be located in different locations. This is opened by clicking the **Open** button on the **Office Button** menu, shown here in Fig. 3.38, or with the **Ctrl+O** keystrokes.

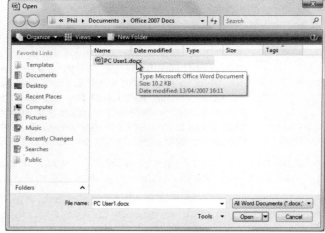

Fig. 3.39 The File Open Box

For example, you can open a document which might be on your computer's hard disc, or on a network drive that you have a connection to. To locate other drives and folders, click the **Computer** item in the Navigation pane, or click on items in the Address bar.

Fig. 3.40 The Vista Address Bar

Having selected the drive and folder within which your document was saved, select its filename and click the **Open** button on the dialogue box.

The last few files you worked on are also listed in the **Office Button** 🕮 menu, as shown in Fig. 3.38 on the facing page. Selecting one of these will reopen that file.

If you do not have any past files displayed, as described above, open the Word Options dialogue box shown in Fig. 3.28, and in the **Display** section of the Advanced tab sheet check the number shown against the **Show this number of Recent Documents** option. You can choose to have up to the last fifty files listed! They will not all be displayed though if there is not room in the window.

New Documents

Fig. 3.41 Part of
Office Button Menu

To start a new document in Word 2007, click the **Office Button** 🕮, and then click the **New** button, as shown here in Fig. 3.41. This opens the New Document window shown below. In the **Templates** list on the left there are options for you to create a blank document, a document from a template installed on your computer, or a new document from an existing file.

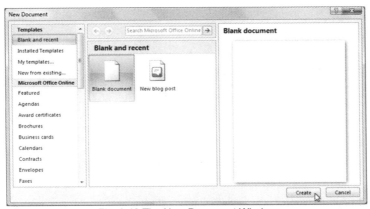

Fig. 3.42 The New Document Window

If you are connected to the Internet, you also see templates that are available from Microsoft Office Online. They have produced 'hundreds' of templates for particular types of documents. These make it very easy for anyone to produce very professional documents. This is well worth exploring.

4

Editing Word Documents

Microsoft have built some very clever editing facilities into Word 2007, and we will introduce some of them here. When you enter text you will notice that some basic errors are automatically corrected and that misspelled words are unobtrusively underlined in a red wavy line and ungrammatical phrases are similarly underlined in green.

AutoCorrect

To demonstrate these, click the **Office Button** , and then click the **New** button, as shown earlier in Fig. 3.41 to create a new document, and type the words '**teh compter is brukn**', exactly as misspelled here.

Fig. 4.1 The AutoCorrect
Options Button

As soon as you press the space bar after entering the first 'word', it will be changed to 'The', as shown in Fig. 4.1. This is the **AutoCorrect** feature at work, which will automatically detect and correct many typing errors, misspelled words, and incorrect capitalisation. If you agree with the change made, as in our example, all is well just carry on. If not, you can move the pointer over the corrected word until a blue box is shown below it. This changes to the **AutoCorrect Options** button when you point to it, and clicking it opens the menu shown above.

Selecting the first menu option **Undo Automatic Corrections** will cancel the correction for you. The other options give you control over how the feature works in the future.

What should appear on your screen is shown in Fig. 4.2, with the two misspelled words underlined in a red wavy line.

Fig. 4.2 Correcting Spelling Mistakes

Right-clicking the first misspelled word allows you to correct it, as shown above. To do this, left-click the **Computer** menu option. You even have a choice of **Language** to use. This is possibly the most time-saving enhancement in editing misspelled words as you type.

During this process the **Status Bar** will indicate your 'state of play'. As shown in Fig. 4.3, the active language is displayed, English (U.K.) in our case. To the left of this, the small 'book' icon has

Fig. 4.3 Status Bar

three forms. In Fig. 4.3 it is ticked to indicate that spell checking is completed. If there are errors to correct, it has a red cross on it 📖, and during the actual checking process it displays an active pencil 📖. If you double-click this icon when it displays a cross, the full spell and grammar checker is opened which will be discussed later in more detail.

If you really have a problem spelling particular words you can add them to the AutoCorrect list yourself. To do this, select the **AutoCorrect** option from the menu in Fig. 4.2 above, or click the **Office Button** 📖, select the **Word Options** command and click **Proofing** followed by **AutoCorrect Options**. These both open the AutoCorrect box shown in Fig. 4.4 on the next page.

Fig. 4.4 Controlling AutoCorrections

The AutoCorrect dialogue box lets you control all of Office 2007's automatic text, formatting and correction features, as well as the Smart Tags feature we will encounter later on. Make sure the AutoCorrect tabbed sheet is active, as shown above, and have a good look at the ways you can control how it works for you. We suggest you scroll through the very long list of common misspellings at the bottom to see which ones will automatically be corrected.

In our example we have chosen to have the program always **Replace** 'compter' **With** the correct spelling of 'computer' as soon as we type the word. Clicking the **Add** button will add these to the AutoCorrect list.

The top fifteen options on the list are not corrections, but give you a rapid way to enter some common symbol characters by typing in a series of keyboard strokes. For example, if you type the three characters '(c)' AutoCorrect will change them to the copyright symbol '©'.

Editing Text

Other editing could include deleting unwanted words or adding extra text in the document. All these operations are very easy to carry out. For small deletions, such as letters or words, the easiest method is to use the **Del** or **BkSp** keys.

With the **Del** key, position the cursor on the left of the first letter you want to delete and press **Del**. With the **BkSp** key, position the cursor immediately to the right of the character to be deleted and press **BkSp**. In both cases the rest of the line moves to the left to take up the space created by the deleting process.

Word processing is usually carried out in the insert mode. Any characters typed will be inserted at the cursor location (insertion point) and the following text will be pushed to the right, and down, to make room. To insert blank lines in your text, place the cursor at the beginning of the line where the blank line is needed and press **Enter**. To remove the blank line, position the cursor on it and press **Del**.

When larger scale editing is needed you have several alternatives. You could first 'select' the text to be altered, then use the **Cut** ✂, **Copy** ⧉ and **Paste** 📋 Ribbon controls in the Clipboard group of the Home tab, as shown here.

Another method of copying or moving text is to use the 'drag and drop' facility which requires you to highlight a word, grab it with the left mouse button depressed, drag it to and drop it in the required place in your text, as shown here in Fig. 4.5.

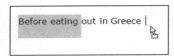

Fig. 4.5 Drag and Drop

These operations will be discussed, in more detail, in the following sections of this chapter.

Selecting Text

The procedure in Word, as with most Windows based applications, is first to select the text to be altered before any operation, such as formatting or editing, can be carried out on it (use the **PC User1** file to experiment). Selected text is highlighted on the screen. This can be carried out in two main ways:

A. *Using the keyboard, to select:*

• A block of text.	Position the cursor on the first character to be selected and hold down the **Shift** key while using the arrow keys to highlight the required text, then release the **Shift** key.
• From the present cursor position to the end of the line.	Use **Shift+End**.
• From the present cursor position to the beginning of the line.	Use **Shift+Home**.
• From the present cursor position to the end of the document.	Use **Shift+Ctrl+End**.
• From the present cursor position to the beginning of the document.	Use **Shift+Ctrl+Home**.
• Select the whole document.	Use **Ctrl A.**

B. With the mouse, to select:

- A block of text.

  Press down the left mouse button at the beginning of the block and while holding it pressed, drag the cursor across the block so that the desired text is highlighted, then release the mouse button.

- A word.

  Double-click within the word.

- A line.

  Place the mouse pointer in the selection bar (just to the left of the line, when it changes to an arrow ⇗) click once. For multiple lines, drag this pointer down.

- A sentence.

  Hold the **Ctrl** key down and click in the sentence.

- A paragraph.

  Place the mouse pointer in the selection bar and double-click (for multiple paragraphs, after selecting the first paragraph, drag the pointer in the selection bar) or triple-click in the paragraph.

- The whole document.

  Place the mouse pointer in the selection bar, hold the **Ctrl** key down and click once.

With Word 2007 you can select non-contiguous text and graphics (ones that aren't next to each other), by selecting the first item you want, such as a word, sentence or paragraph, holding down the **Ctrl** key and selecting any other items from anywhere in the document. You can only select text, or graphics in this way, not both at the same time.

Copying Blocks of Text

Once text has been selected it can be copied to another location in your present document, to another Word document, or to another Windows application, via the system **Clipboard**. As with most of the editing and formatting operations there are several alternative ways of doing this, as follows:

- With the mouse, use the **Copy** 📑 Ribbon control button in the Clipboard group of the Home tab, move the cursor to the start of where you want the copied text to be placed, and click the **Paste** 📋 command.

- With the keyboard, use the quick key combinations, **Ctrl+C** to copy and **Ctrl+V** to paste.

To copy the same text again to another location, or to any open document window or application, move the cursor to the new location and paste it there with either of these methods.

The above operations use the system **Clipboard** which prior to Office XP only held the last item cut or copied. Microsoft Office 2007 comes with a **Clipboard** in which you can store 24 cut or copied items until they are needed. Each item is displayed as an entry on the new **Clipboard** Task Pane as shown in Fig. 4.6 on the next page.

When the Office **Clipboard** Task Pane is active the 📋 icon is added to the Notification Area at the right end of the Windows Taskbar. Moving the pointer over this icon will display the number of items held in the **Clipboard**, whatever Windows application you are currently using.

The Clipboard Task Pane

To illustrate how the **Clipboard** contents can be used, open the **PC User1** file (if not already opened) in Word.

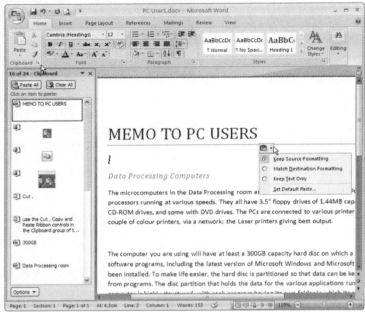

Fig. 4.6 Pasting from the Clipboard Task Pane

Next, select the first line of the memo (in this case "MEMO TO PC USERS") and delete it using either the **Cut** control button in the **Clipboard** group of the **Home** tab, or the **Ctrl+X** key combination. Now open the **Clipboard** Task Pane by clicking the **Clipboard** dialogue box launcher pointed to above. The **Clipboard** Task Pane in Fig. 4.6, shows several text items and graphics. Clicking an item on the **Clipboard**, pastes that item at the cursor position within the memo.

By default a **Smart Tag** button is placed under newly pasted text in Word. Clicking this, as shown above, opens a menu which lets you control the style and formatting of the pasted text. If you don't want to make any formatting changes, just carry on and the smart tag will 'go away'.

Moving Blocks of Text

Selected text can be moved to any location in the same document using either of the following methods:

- Clicking the **Cut** control button.

- Using the **Ctrl+X** keyboard shortcut.

Next, move the cursor to the required new location and as described previously paste the text where you want it.

The moved text will be placed at the cursor location and will force any existing text to make room for it. This operation can be cancelled by simply pressing **Esc**. Once moved, multiple copies of the same text can be produced by other **Paste** actions.

Drag and Drop Operations

 Selected text, or graphics, can be **copied** by holding the **Ctrl** key depressed and dragging the mouse with the left button held down. The copy drag pointer is an arrow with two attached squares, as shown here – the vertical dotted line showing the point of insertion. The new text will insert itself where placed, even if the overstrike mode is in operation. Text copied by this method is not placed on the clipboard, so multiple copies are not possible as with the other methods.

 Selected text can be **moved** by dragging the mouse with the left button held down. The move drag pointer is an arrow with an attached square – the vertical dotted line showing the point of insertion.

Deleting Blocks of Text

When text is 'cut' by clicking the **Cut** control button, it is removed from the document, but placed on the clipboard. When the **Del** or **BkSp** keys are used, however, the text is deleted but not put on the clipboard.

The Undo Command

If you make a mistake when using the delete command, all is not lost as long as you act straight away. The **Undo** keyboard shortcut, **Ctrl+Z,** reverses your most recent editing or formatting commands.

Fig. 4.7 The Undo Button

To make deeper changes you can use the **Undo** button on the Quick Action toolbar, shown here, to undo one of several editing or formatting actions (pressing the down arrow to the right of the button shows a list of your most recent changes).

Undo does not reverse any action once editing changes have been saved to file. Only editing done since the last save can be reversed.

Finding and Changing Text

Word allows you to search for specifically selected text, or character combinations with the **Find** and **Replace** options in the **Editing** group on the **Home** tab of the Ribbon.

Using the **Find** option (**Ctrl+F**), will highlight each occurrence of the supplied text in turn so that you can carry out some action on it, such as change its font or appearance. Using the **Replace** option (**Ctrl+H**), allows you to specify what replacement is to be automatically carried out. For example, in a long article you may decide to replace the word 'microcomputers' with the word 'PCs'.

To illustrate the procedure, click the **Replace** button shown above, (or use the **Ctrl+H** quick key combination). This opens the Find and Replace dialogue box shown on the next page with the **More** button clicked. Towards the bottom of the dialogue box, there are five check boxes; the first two can be used to match the case of letters in the search string, or a whole word, while the last three are used for wildcard, 'sounds like' or 'word forms' matching.

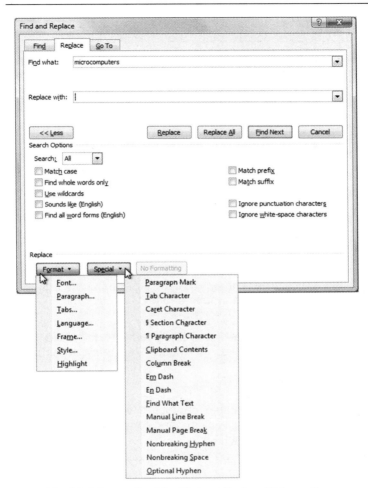

Fig. 4.8 A Composite of the Find and Replace Dialogue Box

The two buttons, **Format** and **Special**, situated at the bottom of the dialogue box, let you control how the search is carried out. The lists of available options, when either of these buttons is pressed, are displayed in Fig. 4.8. You will of course only see one or the other, not both as shown here.

You can force both the search and the replace operations to work with exact text attributes. For example, selecting:

- The **Font** option from the list under **Format**, displays a dialogue box in which you select a font (such as Arial, Times New Roman, etc.); a font-style (such as regular, bold, italic, etc.); an underline option (such as single, double, etc.); and special effects (such as strike-through, superscript, subscript, etc.).

- The **Paragraph** option, lets you control indentation, spacing (before and after), and alignment.

- The **Style** option, allows you to search for, or replace, different paragraph styles. This can be useful if you develop a new style and want to change all the text of another style in a document to use your preferred style.

Using the **Special** button, you can search for, and replace, various specified document marks, tabs, hard returns, etc., or a combination of both these and text, as shown in Fig. 4.8.

Below we list only two of the many key combinations of special characters that could be typed into the **Find what** and **Replace with** boxes when the **Use wildcards** box is checked.

Type	*To find or replace*
?	Any single character within a pattern. For example, searching for nec?, will find <u>neck</u>, con<u>nect</u>, etc.
*	Any string of characters. For example, searching for c*r, will find such words as <u>cellar</u>, <u>chillier</u>, etc., also parts of words such as <u>character</u>, and combinations of words such as <u>connect, cellar</u>.

The Research Task Pane

Clicking the **Review** (Tab), **Proofing** (Group), **Research** button shown here, opens the **Research** Task Pane (Fig. 4.10). This facility is available with all the Office 2007 applications and allows you to reference multiple sources of information, on your computer or the Internet, without leaving an Office program.

For example, you could look up words or phrases in the Encarta Dictionary, which contains over 400,000 entries, and also includes definitions, word histories, pronunciation keys, and word usage notes. Fig. 4.9 below shows the books and research sites that were available to us.

Fig. 4.9 Research Reference Sources

Fig. 4.10 The Research Task Pane

Another source of information is the Thesaurus where you could look up synonyms and insert them into your document directly from the Research Task Pane.

In the list of results on the Research Task Pane, you can also click related links that take you to additional information on the Internet. You can also get translations using bilingual dictionaries on your computer or online, or get stock quotes and company information while you work. The choice is yours!

Page Breaks

Word automatically inserts a 'soft' page break in a document when a page of typed text is full. To force a manual, or hard page break, either use the **Ctrl+Enter** keyboard shortcut, or click the **Insert**, **Pages**, **Page Break** command button on the Ribbon.

A series of dots across the page indicates the page break (this can only be seen in **Draft** view with **Show/Hide** paragraph marks set, as pointed to below). In other views, the second paragraph below appears on the next page.

To delete manual page breaks place the cursor on the line of dots, and press the **Del** key, or place the cursor at the beginning of the second page and press the **BkSp** key.

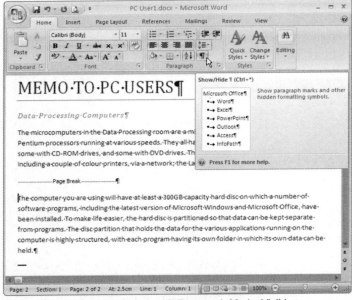

Fig. 4.11 Draft View with Paragraph Marks Visible

Soft page breaks which are automatically entered by the program at the end of pages, cannot be deleted.

Using the Spell Checker

The package has a very comprehensive spell checker which whenever it thinks it has found a misspelled word, underlines it with a red wavy line. To correct your document, right-click such words for alternatives, as we saw earlier.

 However, the spell checker can also be used in another way. To spell check your document, either click the **Review**, **Proofing**, **Spelling & Grammar** button, shown here, or use the **F7** keyboard shortcut to open the dialogue box in Fig. 4.12.

Fig. 4.12 Checking a Whole Document's Spelling

If you want to check a word or paragraph only, highlight it first. Once Word has found a misspelled word, you can either correct it in the **Not in Dictionary:** box, or select a word from the **Suggestions** list and click on **Change**.

If you choose **Add**, the specified word is added to a custom dictionary, which you can edit or add to yourself.

Using the Thesaurus

If you are not sure of the meaning of a word, or you want to use an alternative word in your document, then the

thesaurus is an indispensable tool. Simply place the cursor on the word you want to look up and click the **Review**, **Proofing**, **Thesaurus** button, shown here, or use the **Shift+F7** key combination, to open the Research Task Pane. As long as the word is recognised, synonyms are listed, as shown in Fig. 4.13.

This is a very powerful tool; in our example, you can see information about an item under listings on verbs (v.) and nouns (n.). Selecting a synonym displays a down-arrow against it which, when clicked, produces a drop-down menu of three items. You can choose to **Insert** the selected word in your document in place of the original word, you can **Copy** the selected word to the clipboard so it can be used later, or you can **Look Up** a synonym for this particular word.

You can use the thesaurus like a simple dictionary by typing any word into the **Search for** box and clicking the ⤳ button. Again, if the word is recognised, lists of its meaning variations and synonyms will be displayed.

Fig. 4.13 The Thesaurus

A quick way to get a list of alternatives to a word in your document is to right-click it and select **Synonyms** from the drop-down menu. If you select one from the list it will replace the original word. The last choice in the list activates the **Thesaurus**.

The Grammar Checker

We find the Grammar Checker provided with Word to be much better than that of previous versions of the package. It does not have all the pre-set styles that we are sure were never used by anyone.

To illustrate using the Grammar Checker, open the **PC User1** file (if not already opened) and at the end of it type the following sentence which we know will cause some reaction from the grammar checker.

'Use the Computer utility which Microsoft have spent much time and effort making as intuitive as possible.'

Straight away the Grammar Checker underlines the word 'have' with a green wavy line. Right-clicking the wavy line opens a shortcut menu and choosing the **Grammar** option displays the following:

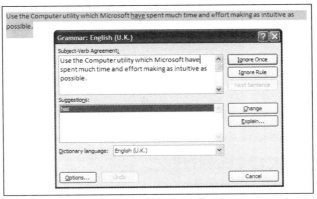

Fig. 4.14 The Grammar Checker

The Grammar Checker has picked up what is incorrect. As expected it prefers 'has' to 'have', just press the **Change** button to make the correction. No other errors were flagged up. Gone are the messages about 'Passive Verb Usage' which was the obsession of the Grammar Checker in some of the older versions of Word. If you want more information on the suggested changes, try clicking the **Explain** button.

To see the spelling and grammar settings in Word 2007, click the **Office Button** 🏛️, select the **Word Options** command and click the **Proofing** tab to open the box shown in Fig. 4.15 below.

Fig. 4.15 Word's Proofing Options

As you can see, you can to a certain extent customise the way the grammar checker works. For example, clicking the

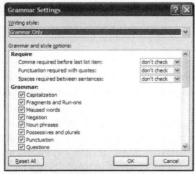

Fig. 4.16 Grammar Settings

Settings button in the screen of Fig. 4.15, displays the Grammar Settings dialogue box shown in Fig. 4.16 where you can make a whole range of choices.

Do spend some time with these two dialogue boxes to find out all the available options before going on.

Printing Documents

When Windows was first installed on your computer the printers you intend to use should have been selected, and the SETUP program should have installed the appropriate printer drivers. Before printing for the first time, it may be a good idea to check that your printer is in fact properly installed. To do this, click the Windows **Start** button (at the left end of the Taskbar) and click **Control Panel** and select **Printers** to open the folder shown in Fig. 4.17.

Fig. 4.17 The Windows Vista Printers Folder

Here, several printer drivers have been installed with the HP LaserJet as the 'default' printer and an Acrobat PDF 'printer' which we often use. In our case the printers are configured to output via USB ports – yours will probably be the same, but could be via the parallel port LPT1. LPT1 is short for Line Printer 1 and refers to the socket at the back of your PC which can be connected to your printer. Similarly, USB ports are also sockets found on your PC or Laptop.

To see how a printer is configured (whether to print to a printer port or to a file), right-click its icon, select **Properties** from the context menu and click the Ports tab of the displayed dialogue box.

Next, return to or reopen Word and, if the document you want to print is not in memory, click the **Open** button on the **Office Button** menu, or use the **Ctrl+O** keystrokes, then use the displayed Open dialogue box to locate and open the file, or document, you want to print, which will be found on the drive and folder on which you saved it originally.

Fig. 4.18 Print Menu Options

To print your document, first click the **Office Button** , and then click the **Print** button to open the sub-menu shown in Fig. 4.18.

Click the **Quick Print** option to print the document using the default printer and current settings.

Use the **Print** option to open the Print dialogue box, shown in Fig. 4.19.

The settings in the Print dialogue box allow you to select the number of copies, and which pages, you want printed. You can also select to print the document, the summary information relating to that document, comments, styles, etc., in the **Print what** drop-down list.

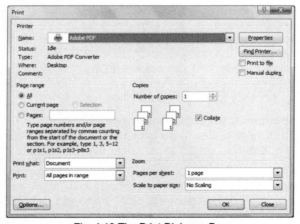

Fig. 4.19 The Print Dialogue Box

You can even change the selected printer by clicking the down arrow against the **Name** box which displays the available printers on your system.

Clicking the **Properties** button on the Print box, displays the Properties dialogue box for the selected printer which allows you to select the paper size, orientation needed, paper source, page order, etc.

The **Options** button on the Print dialogue box, gives you access to some more advanced print options.

Clicking the **OK** button on these various multilevel dialogue boxes, accepts your selections and returns you to the previous level dialogue box, until the Print dialogue box is reached. Selecting **OK** on this first level box, sends print output from Word to your selection, either the printer connected to your computer or in a network, or to an encoded file on disc. Selecting **Cancel** or **Close** on any level dialogue box, aborts the selections made at that level.

Note: One thing to remember is that, whenever you change printers, the appearance of your document may change, as Word uses the fonts available with the newly selected printer. This can affect the line lengths, which in turn will affect both the tabulation and pagination of your document.

Print Preview

Before printing your document to paper, click the **Print Preview** button shown in Fig. 4.18, to see what your print output will look like, and how much of your document will fit on your selected page size. This depends very much on the chosen font. In Fig. 4.20 on the next page we show a preview of our example document PC Users1.doc.

This view allows you to see the layout of the final printed page, which could save a few trees and equally important to you, a lot of frustration, ink and wear and tear on your printer!

The print Preview window has its own Ribbon with **Page Setup** options, **Zoom** viewing options for magnification and number of pages actually shown, and various **Preview** options. The pointer is set as a magnifier by default, but if you turn this off, you can actually edit the text in the Preview window.

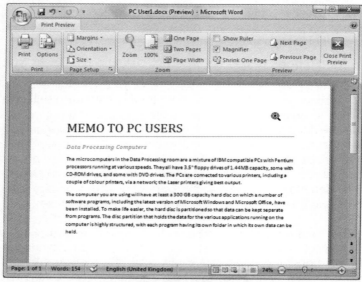

Fig. 4.20 The Print Preview Window

To print the document simply click the **Print** button. To make last minute printer changes click the **Options** button, or to return to your working document click the **Close Print Preview** button. This is a very powerful facility.

5

Formatting Word Documents

Formatting involves the appearance of individual words or even characters, the line spacing and alignment of paragraphs, and the overall page layout of the entire document. These functions are carried out in Word in several different ways.

Primary page layout is included in a document's Template, text formatting in a Template's styles and Theme. Within any document, however, you can override Paragraph Style formats by applying text formatting and enhancements manually to selected text. To immediately cancel manual formatting, use the **Undo** button 🔄 on the Quick Access toolbar, or (**Ctrl+Z**). The text reverts to its original format. In the long term, you can cancel manual formatting by selecting the text and using the **Clear All** option in the Styles Task Pane, as shown in Fig. 3.21 on page 45. The text then reverts to the Normal style format.

Formatting Text

If you use TrueType fonts, which are automatically installed when you set up Windows, Word uses the same font to display text on the screen and to print on paper. The TrueType screen fonts provide a very close approximation of printed characters. TrueType font names are preceded by ᴛᴛ in the Font lists on the Ribbon and Mini Toolbar.

If you use non-TrueType fonts, then use a screen font that matches your printer font. If a matching font is not available, or if your printer driver does not provide screen font information, Windows chooses the screen font that most closely resembles the printer font.

Originally, the title and subtitle of the **PC User1** memo, were selected from the Style gallery and Task Pane as 'Title' and 'Subtitle', which were in the Theme fonts, 26 and 12 point Cambria, respectively, while the main text was typed in 11 point size Calibri.

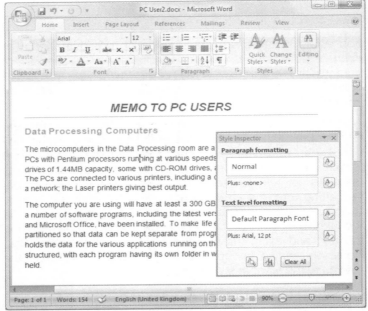

Fig. 5.1 The Reformatted Memo with the Style Inspector

To change this memo into what appears in Fig. 5.1 above, first select the title of the memo and format it to bold, italics, 18 point size Arial and centre it between the margins, then select the subtitle and format it to 14 point size bold Arial. Finally select both paragraphs of the main body of the memo, and format it to 12 point size Arial.

All of this formatting can be achieved by using the buttons on the Ribbon or the Mini Toolbar (see also the section entitled 'Paragraph Alignment'). Save the result under the new filename **PC User2**, using the **Office Button**, **Save As, Word Document** command (Fig. 3.29).

You can examine the style and formatting of any text in the Style Inspector, shown open in Fig. 5.1. This is opened by clicking the **Style Inspector** button at the bottom of the **Styles** Task Bar.

Text Enhancements

In Word all manual formatting, including the selection of font, point size, style (bold, italic, highlight, strike-through, hidden and capitals), colour, super/subscript, spacing and various underlines, are carried out by first selecting the text and then executing the formatting command.

With most actions the easiest way of activating the formatting commands is from the Mini Toolbar, shown to the left in Fig. 5.2 below, or the Ribbon **Home**, **Font** controls shown to the right below.

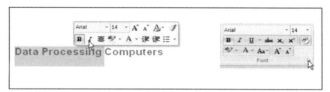

Fig. 5.2 Mini Toolbar (Left) and Ribbon, Home, Font (Right)

With others you have to use the Font dialogue box shown in Fig. 5.3 on the next page. This is opened by clicking the **Dialogue Box Launcher** pointed to on the right above.

Yet another method is using keyboard shortcuts, some of which are listed below:

To Format	*Type*
Bold	**Ctrl+B**
Italic	**Ctrl+I**
Underline	**Ctrl+U**
Word underline	**Ctrl+Shift+W**

There are shortcuts to do almost anything, but the ones listed here are the most useful and the easiest to remember.

Fig. 5.4 Paragraph Group

Fig. 5.3 The Font Dialogue Box

Paragraph Alignment

Word defines a paragraph, as any text which is followed by a paragraph mark, which is created by pressing the **Enter** key. So single line titles, as well as sections of long typed text, can form paragraphs.

Word allows you to align a paragraph at the left margin (the default), at the right margin, centred between both margins, or justified between both margins.

There are two main ways to perform alignment in Word. Using the **Home**, **Paragraph** command buttons, shown in Fig. 5.4 above, or using keyboard shortcuts.

Ribbon Buttons	*Alignment*	*Keystrokes*
	Left	**Ctrl+L**
	Centred	**Ctrl+E**
	Right	**Ctrl+R**
	Justified	**Ctrl+J**

Paragraph Spacing

There are two ways to control indents ⊒⊒ and spacing ⊟⊽ in Word. Using the **Home**, **Paragraph** command buttons shown here, or the Paragraph box opened by clicking the **Home**, **Paragraph**, **Dialogue Box Launcher** ⊡.

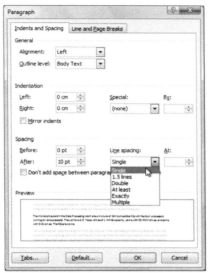

Fig. 5.5 The Paragraph Box

The settings in this box will affect the current paragraph (with the insertion point in it), or any selected paragraphs. Here you can specify any **Left, Right**, or **Special** indentation required, and set your paragraph line spacing to single-line, 1.5 line, or double-line spacing. You can even set the spacing to any value you want by using the **At Least** option, as shown above, then specify what interval you want.

The available shortcut keys for paragraph spacing are as follows:

To Format	Type
Single-spaced lines	**Ctrl+1**
One-and-a-half-spaced lines	**Ctrl+5**
Double-spaced lines	**Ctrl+2**

Whichever of the above methods is used, formatting can take place either before or after the text is entered. If formatting is selected first, then text will type in the chosen format until a further formatting command is given. If, on the other hand, you choose to enter text and then format it afterwards, you must first select the text to be formatted, then activate the formatting.

Fig. 5.6 Line Spacing from the Ribbon

Line spacing can also be controlled from the Ribbon by clicking the down-arrow against the **Page Layout**, **Paragraph**, **Line Spacing** button, shown here, and selecting one of the displayed options.

Word gives you the choice of 5 units to work with, inches, centimetres, millimetres, points or picas. These can be selected in the Word Options box by clicking the **Office Button**, selecting the **Word Options** command, clicking the Advanced tab and scrolling down to the **Display** section shown in Fig. 5.7. We have selected to **Show measurements in units of:** the default centimetres.

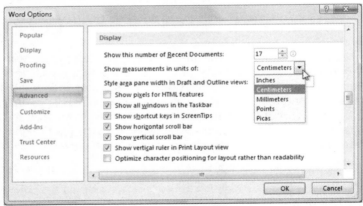

Fig. 5.7 Word 2007's Display Options

Indenting Text

Most documents will require some form of paragraph indenting, where an indent is the space between the margin and the edge of the text in the paragraph. When an indent is set (on the left or right side of the page), any justification on that side of the page sets at the indent, not the page margin.

To illustrate indentation, open the file **PC User2**, select the first paragraph, and open the Paragraph box by clicking the **Home**, **Paragraph**, **Dialogue Box Launcher** . In the **Indentation** field, select 2.5 cm for both **Left** and **Right**, as shown in Fig. 5.8 below. When you click **OK**, the first selected paragraph is displayed indented. Our screen dump shows the result of the indentation as well as the settings on the Paragraph dialogue box which caused it.

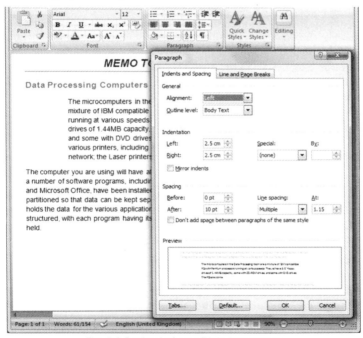

Fig. 5.8 Setting Left and Right Indentation

You can also use the **Home**, **Paragraph**, **Indent** buttons to decrease or increase left indents.

The **Indentation** option in the Paragraph dialogue box, can be used to create 'hanging' indents, where all the lines in a paragraph, including any text on the first line that follows a tab, are indented by a specified amount. This is often used in lists to emphasise certain points.

To illustrate the method, use the **PC User1** file and add at the end of it the text shown below. After you have typed the text in, save the enlarged memo as **PC User3**, before going on with formatting the new text.

In Windows you can work with files in three different ways:

Name Description

My Computer Use the My Computer utility from the Start menu, which Microsoft has spent much time and effort making as intuitive as possible.

Explorer Use the Windows Explorer from the Start, All Programs, Accessories sub-menu.

MS-DOS Use the Command Prompt window from the Start, All Programs, Accessories sub-menu, if you prefer to and are an expert with the DOS commands.

Fig. 5.9 Additional Text to be Typed in Word

Saving the work at this stage is done as a precaution in case anything goes wrong with the formatting – it is sometimes much easier to reload a saved file, than it is to try to unscramble a wrongly formatted document!

Next, highlight the last four paragraphs above, open the Paragraph dialogue box, and select 'Hanging' under **Special** and 3 cm under **By**. When you click the **OK** button, the text formats as shown in the composite screen dump of Fig. 5.10, but it is still highlighted. To remove the highlighting, click the mouse button anywhere on the page. The second and following lines of the selected paragraphs, should be indented 3 cm from the left margin.

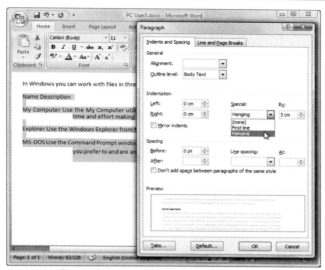

Fig. 5.10 Setting Hanging Indents Manually

This is still not very inspiring, so to complete the effect we will edit the first lines of each paragraph as follows:

Place the cursor in front of the word 'Description' and press the **Tab** key once. This places the start of the word in the same column as the indented text of the other paragraphs. To complete the effect place tabs before the words 'Use' in the next three paragraphs, until your hanging indents are correct, as shown in Fig. 5.11 below. To make more room, we have hidden the Ribbon (see page 24).

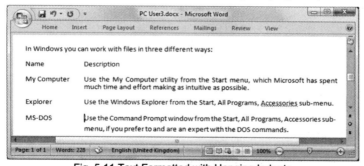

Fig. 5.11 Text Formatted with Hanging Indents

This may seem like a complicated rigmarole to go through each time you want the hanging indent effect, but with Word you will eventually set up all your indents, etc., as styles in templates. Then all you do is click in a paragraph to produce them. We will discuss this towards the end of this chapter.

Adding a Drop Capital

Another text feature that you may want to use at times is to make the first letter of a paragraph a large dropped initial capital letter, as shown here.

With Word that is ridiculously easy. Just place the insertion point at the beginning of the existing paragraph and click the **Insert**, **Text**, **Drop Cap** command arrow ▼. This opens the drop-down menu shown in Fig. 5.12 below.

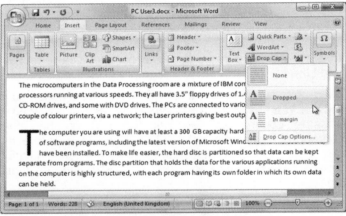

Fig. 5.12 Setting a Dropped Capital Letter

You can choose between **Dropped** and **In margin** for the position of the initial capital letter. For more control you can select **Drop Cap Options**. You can then change the **Font**, select how many **Lines to drop** and set the **Distance from text**.

The new first letter is actually a graphic image. To remove the effect if you decide you don't want it, select the image by clicking it, and select **None** from the **Drop Cap** drop-down menu.

When you finish formatting the document, save it under its current filename by clicking the **Save** button on the Quick Access toolbar. This command does not display a dialogue box, so you use it when you do not need to make any changes during the saving operation.

Bullets and Lists

Bullets are small characters you can insert in the text of your document to improve visual impact. In Word the main way for creating lists with bullets or numbers is from the Ribbon, **Home**, **Paragraph** group. Clicking the **Bullets** ≔ button, the **Numbering** ≔ button or the **Multilevel List** button will start the operation. You can change the bullet or list design used by clicking the down-arrow next to its button. If none of the available designs appeal to you, you can create your own by clicking **Define New Bullet** at the bottom of the box, as shown in Fig. 5.13 below.

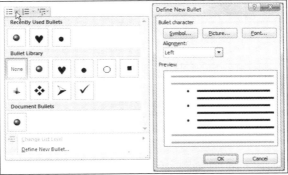

Fig. 5.13 Selecting and Defining Bullets

There are two types of bullet you can define. Clicking the **Symbol** button above lets you use a character from a font, whereas **Picture** bullets are just small graphic images. With the latter option you can select from an enormous number of bullet pictures. Very comprehensive.

If you select he **Numbering** ≔ button or the **Multilevel List** button similar options are displayed, giving you a choice of several numbering or outline (multilevel) systems.

Once inserted, you can copy, move or cut a bulleted paragraph in the same way as any other text. However, you can not delete a bullet with the **BkSp** or **Del** keys. To do this, you need to place the insertion point in the line and click the **Bullets** ⊞ ▾ button, shown here. Once you have set up a customised bullet, clicking this button in a paragraph will use it.

Note: If you only want a simple list you can create it without using the Ribbon buttons. For a bulleted list, just type an asterisk '*' followed by a space. The asterisk turns into a bullet and your list is started. When you've finished typing the first item in your list, press the **Enter** key and a new bullet will appear on the next line.

To automatically create numbered lists in a similar way, type the number one and a full stop '**1.**', followed by a space.

When you have finished entering your list, pressing the **Enter** key twice will close it. Every time you press the **Enter** key at the end of the list you get a new bullet or number, but if you press it again, the last bullet or number disappears.

You can use the following symbols to create automatic bulleted lists:

-	One minus sign
--	Two minus signs
-> or -->	One or two minus signs and a close angle bracket
=> or ==>	One or two equal signs and a close angle bracket
<>	Open and close angle brackets
>	Close angle bracket
Letter **o**	Followed by a tab, not a space.

To format bullets or numbers separately from the text in the list, just click one of the bullets or numbers to select them all. You can then format them the same as any other text by using the commands on the Ribbon.

Well worth experimenting here.

Inserting Date and Time

You can insert today's date, the date the current document was created or was last revised, or a date or time that reflects the current system date and time into a document. Therefore, the date can be a date that changes, or a date that always stays the same. In either case, the date is inserted in a date field.

To insert a date field in your document, place the cursor where you want to insert the date, click the **Insert**, **Text**, **Date & Time** button 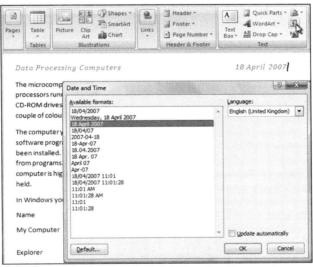 and choose one of the displayed date formats from the dialogue box shown in Fig. 5.14 below. This is a composite of the operation required and the result of that operation.

Fig. 5.14 Inserting Dates and Times in a Document

If you save a document with a date field in it and you open it a few days later, the date shown on it will be the original date the document was created. Most of the time this will probably be what you want, but should you want the displayed date to always update to the current date whenever the document is opened, check the **Update automatically** box, and then click the **OK** button.

Comments and Tracked Changes

Another of Word's powerful features is the facility to add comments and to track changes made to a document. These actions are all carried out from the **Review** tab.

Comments are notes, or annotations, that an author or reviewer adds to a document and in Word 2007 they are displayed in balloons in the margin of the document or in the Reviewing Pane. A tracked change is a mark that shows where a deletion, insertion, or other editing change has been made in a document.

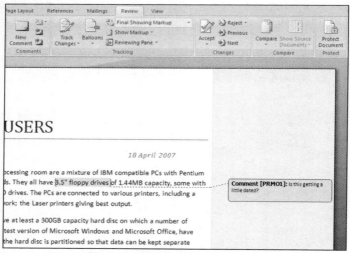

Fig. 5.15 A Comment in a Document

To quickly display or hide tracked changes or comments (known as markup) click the **Review**, **Tracking**, **Show Markup** command button, and select what you want to display on the screen. To add a comment, place the pointer in the correct location, click the **New Comment** button, and type the comment into the 'balloon' that opens in the margin. You can view a document's markup by clicking the **Reviewing Pane** command button. You can print a document with markup to keep a record of any changes made.

Formatting with Page Tabs

You can format text in columns by using tab stops placed on the Ruler, opened by clicking the **View Ruler** button. Although they are not shown on the Ruler, but as small marks below it, Word has default left tab stops at 1.27 cm intervals. The symbol for a left tab appears in the tab type button at the left edge of the ruler shown in Fig 5.16 below.

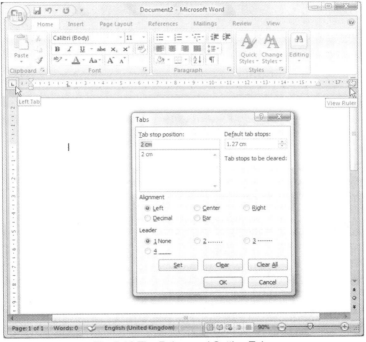

Fig. 5.16 The Rulers and Setting Tabs

To set tabs, click on the tab type button (which cycles through the available types) until the type you want is showing and then click on the ruler. To remove a tab, just drag it off the ruler.

To place tabs exactly, first set one on the Ruler and then double-click it to open the Tabs dialogue box shown above.

Type the distance from the left margin for your tab in the **Tab stop position** text box and click the **Set** button. To clear the ruler of tabs press the **Clear All** button. To remove one tab, select it in the list and click the **Clear** button. Tab stops apply either to the paragraph containing the cursor, or to any selected paragraphs.

The tab stop types available have the following functions:

Button	*Name*	*Effect*
L	**Left**	Left aligns text after the tab stop.
⊥	**Centre**	Centres text on tab stop.
⌐	**Right**	Right aligns text at the tab stop.
⊥.	**Decimal**	Aligns decimal point with tab stop.
I	**Bar**	Inserts a vertical line at the tab stop.

The tab type button actually cycles through two more types, first line indent ▽ and hanging indent ⌐. These give you a quick way of adding these indents to the ruler.

If you want tabular text to be separated by characters instead of by spaces, select one of the four available characters from the **Leader** box in the Tabs dialogue box. The options are none (the default), dotted, dashed and underline. The Contents pages of this book are set with right tabs and dotted leader characters.

When you are finished click the **OK** button to make your changes active. Now using the Tab key displays the selected leader characters. If you don't like what you see, press the **Clear All** button in the Tabs dialogue box. This will take you back to the default Tab settings.

Note: As all paragraph formatting, such as tab stops, is placed at the end of a paragraph, if you want to carry the formatting of the current paragraph to the next, press **Enter**. If you don't want formatting to carry on, press the down arrow key instead.

Formatting with Styles

We saw earlier on page 44, how you can format your work using Quick Styles, but we confined ourselves to using the default styles only. In this section we will give an overview of how to create, modify, use, and manage styles. Word's Style controls, shown here, are in the **Home**, **Styles** group.

A Style is a set of formatting instructions which you save so that you can use it repeatedly within a document or in different documents. A collection of Styles can be placed in a Template which could be appropriate for, say, all your memos, so it can be used to preserve uniformity and save time by not having to format each paragraph individually.

Further, should you decide to change a style, all the paragraphs associated with that style can reformat automatically. Finally, if you want to provide a pattern for shaping a final document, then you use what is known as a Template. By default all documents which have not been assigned a template, use the **Normal.dotm** global template.

Paragraph Styles

Styles contain paragraph and character formats and a name can be attached to these formatting instructions. From then on, applying the style name is the same as formatting that paragraph with the same instructions.

With Word you can create your styles by example from the **Styles** Task Pane, shown here in Fig. 5.17, which is opened by clicking the **Dialogue Box Launcher** on the **Home**, **Styles** group.

Fig. 5.17 Styles Task Pane

Creating a New Paragraph Style: Previously, we spent some time manually creating some hanging indents in the last few paragraphs of the **PC User3** document. Open that document and display the **Styles** Task Pane. Place the insertion pointer in one of the previously created hanging indent paragraphs, say, in the 'Name Description' line and click the **New Style** button ▦ pointed to below.

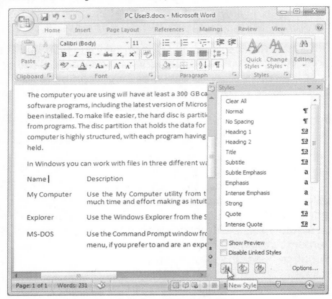

Fig. 5.18 Creating a New Style

This opens the dialogue box shown in Fig. 5.20 on the next page. Now type the new style name you want to create in the **Name** text box, say, 'Hanging Indent', then select the **Add to Quick Style list** option at the bottom of the box, and click **OK** to accept your changes.

Finally, change the style of the other paragraphs to the new 'Hanging Indent', by selecting the new style either from the list in the **Styles** Task Pane, or more easily,

Fig. 5.19 New Quick Style

from the **Quick Styles** gallery as shown in Fig. 5.19 above.

Fig. 5.20 Creating a New Style from Formatting

Save the result as **PC User4**, make yourself a drink, and relax – you have earned it!

Before leaving this section. have a look at some more of Word's built-in styles by clicking the **Home**, **Styles**, **Change Styles** command button, shown in Fig. 5.21.

Fig. 5.21 The Change Styles Theme Options

There are lots of available styles, one of which might suit you. We will leave you to try them yourself, though.

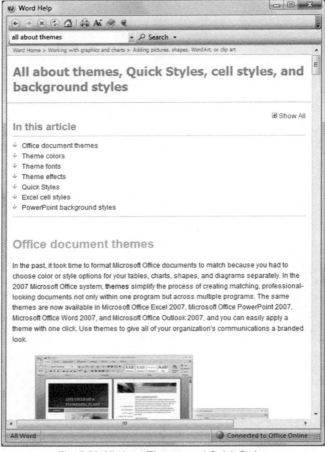

Fig. 5.22 All about Themes and Quick Styles

If you want some help on the **Change Styles** options, try searching for the above document in the Word Help system. To find it we searched for:

All about themes

You will need to be online though, as it is part of Office Online.

Document Templates

A document template provides the overall pattern of your final document. It can contain:

- Styles to control your paragraph and formats.

- A Theme to control document colours and fonts.

- Page set-up options.

- Boilerplate text, which is text that remains the same in every document.

- AutoText, which is standard text and graphics that you could insert in a document by typing the name of the AutoText entry.

- Macros, which are programs that can change the menus and key assignments to comply with the type of document you are creating.

- Customised shortcuts, toolbars and menus.

If you don't assign a template to a document, then the default **Normal.dotx** template is used by Word. To create a new document template, you either modify an existing one, create one from scratch, or create one based on the formatting of an existing document.

Creating a Document Template

To illustrate the last point above, we will create a simple document template, which we will call **PC User**, based on the formatting of the **PC User4** document. But first, make sure you have defined the 'Hanging Indent' style as explained earlier.

To create a template based on an existing document do the following:

- Open the existing document.

- Select the **Office Button, Save As, Word Template** command which displays the Save As dialogue box, shown in Fig. 5.23.

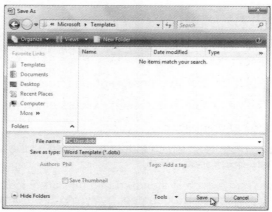
Fig. 5.23 Saving a Document as a Template

- In the list on the left, click **Templates** (Vista), or **Trusted Templates** (XP) to open the Templates folder.

- In the **File name** box, type the name of the new template (PC User in our example).

- Press the **Save** button, which opens the template file **PC User.dotx** in the Word working area for you to edit.

- Add the text and graphics you want to appear in all new documents that you base on this template, and *delete* any items (including text) you do not want to appear.

Fig. 5.24 Artwork and Text in the New Template

In our example, we deleted everything in the document, bar the heading, and added the words 'PC User Group' using **Insert**, **Text**, **WordArt**, as above.

- Click the **Save** button on the Quick Access toolbar, and close the document.

To use the new template, do the following:

- Use the **Office Button**, **New** command and select **My templates** from the list. This opens the New dialogue box with access to the My Templates folder, as shown in Fig. 5.25 below.

Fig. 5.25 New Template in the My Templates Folder

- Select the name of the template you want to use from the displayed list. This would be **PCUser.dotx** in our case.

- Make sure that the radio button **Document** is selected, and click the **OK** button.

The new document opened will be using the selected template.

Templates can also contain Macros as well as AutoText; macros allow you to automate Word keystroke actions only, while AutoText speeds up the addition of 'Building Blocks' text and graphics into your document. However, the design of these features is beyond the scope of this book.

Don't forget that Word has a series of built-in templates to suit 'every occasion'.

The Default Character Format

As we have seen, for all new documents Word 2007 uses the Calibri type font with 11 points size as the default for the Normal style, which is contained in the Normal template. If the majority of your work demands some different font style or size, then you can change these defaults.

To change the default font, open the Font dialogue box shown in Fig. 5.26, by clicking the **Home**, **Font**, **Dialogue Box Launcher** 🔲. Then select the new defaults you want to use, and click the **Default** button.

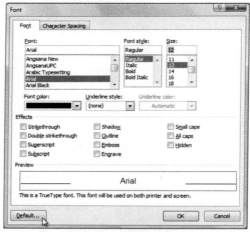

Fig. 5.26 Setting a New Default Font

A warning box opens to make sure you really know what you are about to do. Pressing the **Yes** button, changes the default character settings for this and all subsequent new documents using the Normal template, but does not change already existing ones. Pressing **No** aborts the operation.

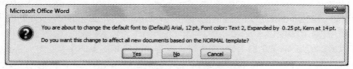

Fig. 5.27 A Warning Message Box

Symbols and Special Characters

Word 2007 lets you easily add symbols to your documents. Clicking the **Insert**, **Symbols**, **Symbol** command button shown below, opens a small gallery of common and recently used symbols for you to choose from. Clicking the **More Symbols** option on this opens the Symbol dialogue box shown in Fig. 5.28 below. From this you can select characters and symbols and insert them into your document.

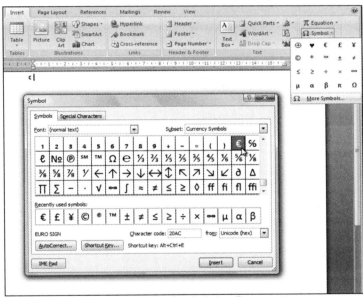

Fig. 5.28 Inserting Symbols in a Document

You should be able to find just about any symbol you require in the Symbol font box shown above. But if not, pressing the down-arrow button next to the **Font** box, will reveal the other available character sets. If you double-click the left mouse button on a character, it transfers it to your document at the insertion point.

The **AutoCorrect** button opens the box shown in Fig. 4.4 (page 63) so that you can insert any of the symbols in the **Replace text as you type** section.

Inserting Other Special Characters

You can include other special characters in a document, such as optional hyphens, which remain invisible until they are needed to hyphenate a word at the end of a line; non-breaking hyphens, which prevent unwanted hyphenation; non-breaking spaces, which prevent two words from splitting at the end of a line; or opening and closing single quotes.

There are two ways to insert these special characters in your document. One is to click the **Special Characters** tab of the Symbol dialogue box which reveals a long list of these special characters, as shown in Fig. 5.29 below. You then select one of them and click the **Insert** button.

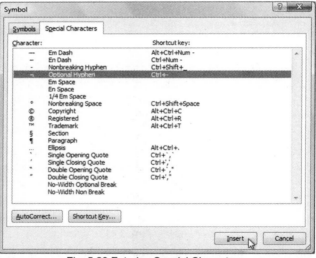

Fig. 5.29 Entering Special Characters

The other way is to use the keyboard shortcut key combinations listed above in Fig. 5.29, which does not require you to open the dialogue box. But you do have to remember them though!

6

Document Enhancements

In this section we discuss features that can enhance a document's appearance, such as page numbering, using headers and footers, or footnotes, how to create a document with multiple columns, how to incorporate text boxes, how to use pictures and graphics, and how to build equations.

Page Numbering

If you need to number the pages of a document you use the **Insert**, **Header & Footer**, **Page Number** command button, and click **Top of Page**, **Bottom of Page**, or **Page Margins**, depending on where you want page numbers to appear in your document. Then choose a page numbering design from the gallery of designs shown in Fig. 6.2 on the next page.

Fig. 6.1 Number Formats

Clicking the **Format Page Numbers** option, opens the Page Number Format box we show here in Fig. 6.1.

From this box you can select the **Number format** from the following alternatives, '1, – 1 –, a, A, i, or I'; the more usual style being the first option, as used in this book.

Page numbering gives you two alternatives; **Continue from previous section**, or **Start at** a specified number. Some explanation is needed here.

Fig. 6.2 The Page Numbers Gallery

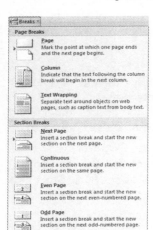

With Word you can split a document up into different sections, with each section having different page formats, headers and footers or page numbering. You do this by adding section breaks with the **Page Layout**, **Page Setup**, **Breaks** button menu shown in Fig. 6.3.

Fig. 6.3 Page and Section Breaks

To illustrate page numbering, open the **PC Users4** document, click the **Insert**, **Header & Footer**, **Page Number** command, select **Bottom of Page** and click the **Plain Number 2** option from the opened gallery (Fig. 6.2). The result is a number '1' appearing centrally in a footer at the bottom of page 1, as shown in Fig. 6.4 below. It is selected and the **Header & Footer Tools**, **Design** tab is opened for you to make any changes you want.

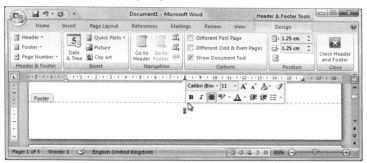

Fig. 6.4 A Page Number with the Header & Footer Design Tab

To change the page numbering style, click the **Header & Footer**, **Page Number** button, shown above, and then select **Format Page Numbers**. In the Page Number Format box of Fig. 6.1, click a numbering style, and then click **OK**.

To change the font and size of page numbers, select a page number and make your choices on the Mini toolbar that appears above the selected number as shown in Fig. 6.4.

To return to the main document, either double-click in it, or click the **Close Header and Footer** button ⊠. If you double-click in the Footer area it will be re-opened ready for editing with the **Header & Footer Tools**, **Design** tab.

Finally, save the current document as **PC Users5**.

Using Headers and Footers

Headers consist of text placed in the top margin area of a page, whereas footers are text in the bottom margin. Simple headers or footers in Word can consist of text and a page number, which are produced in the same position of every page in a document, while more complicated ones can also contain graphics or logos.

Word allows you to have one header/footer for the first page of a document, or section of a document, and different ones for the rest of the document. It also allows you to select a different header or footer for odd or even pages.

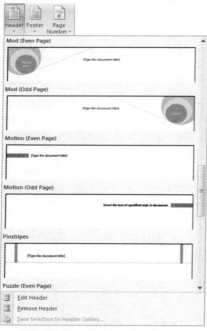

You can insert pre-designed headers or footers into your document from the gallery, and then easily change them to whatever you want. Or you can create your own, say with your company logo and a custom look, and save them to the gallery for future use.

To insert a header or footer in a document, first click the **Insert**, **Header & Footer**, **Header** (or **Footer)** button and then select from the gallery which opens, shown here in Fig. 6.5.

Fig. 6.5 Part of the Header Gallery

The header or footer is created at the top or bottom of the document, and the **Header & Footer Tools**, **Design** tab is opened for you.

Fig. 6.6 A Newly Placed Header from the Gallery

From here, you can use the Ribbon buttons to customise or add your own header information. For example, you can insert a **Page Number** and format it with the Mini toolbar, insert the current **Date & Time**, or a **Picture** such as your logo, or **Clip Art**. You can use the **Options** group buttons to create a different header or footer for the first page of a document, or create different headers and footers for odd and even pages. You can also show and hide the document text, create similar headers and footers in a section to those of a previous section, or jump to the previous or next header and footer.

Headers and footers can be formatted and edited like any other text, but the header or footer area must be 'active'. If you are in the main document area, anything in your headers or footers will be a pale grey colour. In this case, to edit a header or footer, simply point to its panel and double-click in it. The text will go black and the **Header & Footer Tools**, **Design** tab will be opened for you.

You can then use any of the Ribbon tabs, or the buttons on the Mini toolbar to format or edit the header or footer.

To return to the main document, either double-click in it, or click the **Close Header and Footer** button ✖ at the far right of the Ribbon.

Footnotes and Endnotes

If your document requires **footnotes** at the end of each page, or **endnotes** at the end of each chapter, they are very easy to add and later, if necessary, to edit. Place the cursor where you want the reference point to be in the document and select **References**, **Footnotes**, **Insert Footnote** (or **Insert Endnote**) as shown in Fig. 6.7 below.

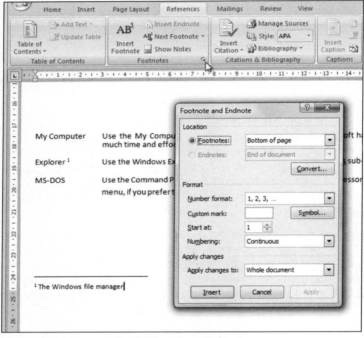

Fig. 6.7 Inserting a Footnote

In Fig. 6.7, the reference point was placed after the word 'Explorer' and the line and reference number were added at the bottom of the page. We then typed the text for the footnote. The dialogue box is opened by clicking the Dialogue Box Launcher pointed to above. In it you can control the process, such as changing the **Number format**, or setting what number to **Start at**.

Using Multiple Columns on a Page

You can quickly modify the number of displayed columns for 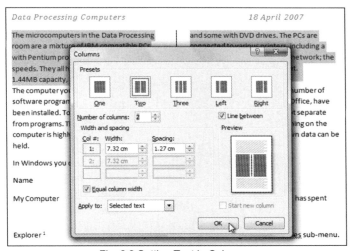a selected part of a document or section by using the **Page layout**, **Page Setup**, **Columns** button, shown here. This lets you select the number of columns, but if you want more control over how the columns are displayed, then use the **More Columns** option to open the Columns box shown in Fig. 6.8 below.

Here we have selected the first paragraph of the **PC Users5** memo and formatted it into two columns with a **Line between**.

Fig. 6.8 Setting Text in Columns

To see how the 'Preview' page changes, click the appropriate button on the **Presets** field of this Columns dialogue box. Now change the **Spacing** (otherwise known as gutter width) to see how to set the separation zones between columns.

In the **Number of columns** box you can choose up to 12 columns. The **Apply to** option controls whether the columns are applied to the text selected, or the rest of the document.

Text Boxes

Text boxes can best be thought of as containers for text that can be positioned on a page and sized independently of the rest of the page. They were first used in Word 97, and can be quite useful. For example, you can make text flow from one part of a document to another part by putting it in text boxes and linking them together.

Inserting Text Boxes

With Word you can create an empty text box by clicking the **Insert**, **Text**, **Text Box** button to open the gallery shown here. There are 36 types of text boxes to choose from, and you can add your own with the **save Selection to Text Box Gallery** option.

When you select one, if you are not in **Page Layout** mode, the program will automatically switch you to it. The new text box will be placed in your document and the **Text Box Tools** tab will open as shown in Fig. 6.10.

When you type text, it wraps to fit the text box, but if you type more lines than will fit in the text box, you will have to increase its vertical size manually to see all the text.

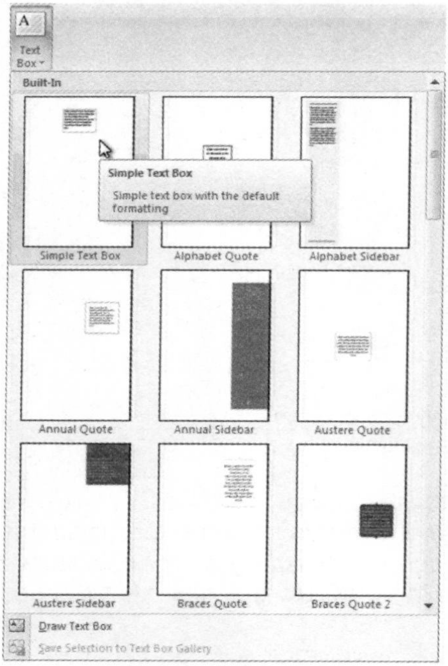

Fig. 6.9 The Text Box Gallery

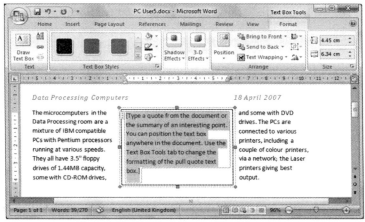

Fig. 6.10 A New Text Box and Text Box Tools

In our example above, we selected a **Simple Text Box** from the gallery, which was added on top of the existing text in the document. We didn't want this, so we clicked the **Text Wrapping** button on the **Text Tools Tab** and selected **Tight**, as shown in Fig. 6.11, to change from the default setting of **In Front of Text**.

Fig. 6.11 Text Wrapping

As shown above, the text box is selected and has a dotted line around it with round 'handles' at each corner and square ones on each side. When you move the pointer over these handles it changes shape to 🖑, ⇔ or ⬈. You can re-size the box by dragging these handles, up or down, left or right, or diagonally.

To move a text box around your document first select it, then move the mouse pointer over its edge until it turns to a four-headed arrow, then click and drag to the desired position, as shown here. The dotted outline shows the position in which the frame will be placed once you let go of the mouse button.

Fig. 6.12 Text Box Positioning

Another way of positioning a text box is by first selecting it, then clicking the **Text Box Tools**, **Position** button to display the gallery position options shown in Fig. 6.12. As you move the pointer over the gallery options your document will preview each option in turn. To accept one just click it.

Selecting **More Layout Options** from below the gallery, opens the Advanced Layout dialogue box, shown below in Fig. 6.13.

In this box you can specify the exact position of the text box. You also have the option of anchoring the box in that exact position, or allowing it to move with the document text.

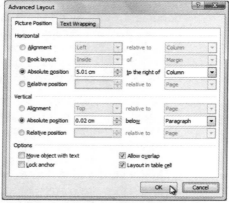

Fig. 6.13 Controlling the Layout of a Text Box

Pressing the Text Wrapping tab of the Advanced Layout dialogue box above, opens the one shown in Fig. 6.14 on the facing page. This allows you to specify the wrapping options when a text box is placed in the middle of an existing paragraph. If you select a wrapping style other than **Top & bottom**, then format the text into two columns before inserting the text box – it will look much better.

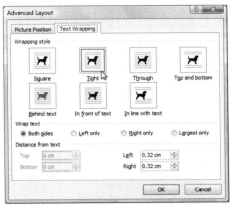

Fig. 6.14 Controlling Text Wrapping Options

Wrapping style options can be selected in the above Advanced Layout dialogue box, or by clicking the **Text Wrapping** button on the **Text Tools Tab** shown earlier in Fig. 6.11.

The **Text** group on the **Text Tools Tab**, shown here, allows you to create and break forward text box links, to go to the previous and next text box, change text direction and draw a new text box by dragging the pointer.

Rotating Text in a Text Box

With some of the preformed text boxes in the gallery, once you have placed them with their contents where you want on the page, you can rotate them, using the **Text Box Tools**, **Arrange**, **Rotate** button .

Note: You can select a text box at any time by clicking it, and either re-size or move it, and if you clicked anywhere in the text within the text box, you can also edit that.

Inserting Illustrations

Word 2007 has very much improved graphics rendering features, accessed from the **Illustrations** group on the **Insert** tab, shown here. You can insert pictures, clip art, shapes, SmartArt and charts or graphs.

Inserting Pictures

In Fig. 6.15 below we clicked the **Insert**, **Illustrations**, **Picture** button and selected a photograph from the Sample Pictures folder that was offered, but we could have browsed for any image file on our computer. The image was placed inline, at the cursor position, and the **Picture Tools**, **Format** tab was opened, as shown below.

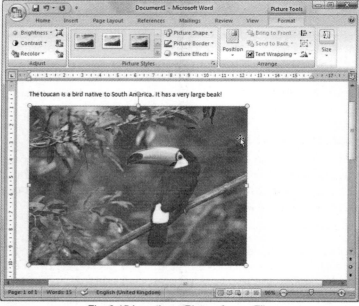

Fig. 6.15 Inserting a Picture from a File

To insert a picture from a Web page or other document, first right-click it and select **Copy** from the context menu. Then position the cursor where you want the picture and click the **Home**, **Clipboard**, **Paste** button.

By default, Word embeds pictures in a document and places them inline with the text, so that you cannot move them around the document. You can change an inline picture to a floating one where it is inserted in the drawing layer so that you can position it precisely on the page or in front of or behind text or other objects.

To do this, select the picture and click the **Picture Tools**, **Format**, **Arrange**, **Position** button, and select the wrapping style that you want, as shown earlier in Fig. 6.12.

Another way is to click the **Picture Tools**, **Format**, **Arrange**, **Text Wrapping** button and select a wrapping style such as **Tight**, as shown in Fig. 6.16. The default setting is **In Line with Text**.

| Text Wrapping ▾ |
| ☒ In Line with Text |
| ☒ Square |
| ☒ Tight |
| ☒ Behind Text |
| ☒ In Front of Text |
| ☒ Top and Bottom |
| ☒ Through |
| ☒ Edit Wrap Points |
| ☐ More Layout Options... |

Fig. 6.16 Text Wrapping

When a picture is selected by being clicked it has round handles at each corner and square ones on each side. When you move the pointer over these handles it changes shape to ⇕, ⇔ or ↗. You can re-size the picture by dragging these handles.

To move a picture around your document first select it, then if necessary change its text wrapping, and then move the mouse pointer over its edge until it turns to a four-headed arrow, then click and drag the picture to the desired position, as shown here in Fig. 6.17. The 'pale image' shows the position in which the frame will be placed once you let go of the mouse button.

Fig. 6.17 Moving a Picture

The Picture Tools Ribbon

When a picture is selected in a Word document the **Picture Tools**, **Format** ribbon tab is opened, as shown in Fig. 6.18.

Fig. 6.18 The Picture Tools, Format Ribbon Tab

This gives a range of tools that can be used to manipulate the picture to suit your needs. Try using these tools on an imported image to see how you can enhance or utterly destroy it! If, at the end of the day, you don't save it, it doesn't matter what you do to it. Just experiment.

In Fig. 6.19 below we inserted a photograph of our Westie, and while it was selected in the document, used two of the tools available on the **Picture Tools**, **Format** tab.

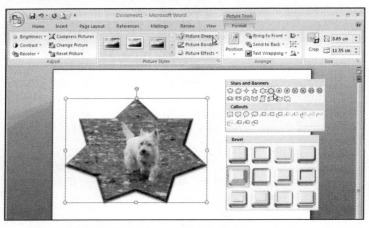

Fig. 6.19 Using Picture Shape and Picture Effects

First we clicked the **Picture Shape** button, pointed to above, and selected a 7-point star from the Stars and Banners section. Then we clicked the **Picture Effects** button and selected a Bevel. The range of Picture Tools available is enormous though, and we defy anyone not to find something useful here. Some of the drop shadow effects are excellent.

Cropping a Picture

Cropping reduces the size of a picture by removing vertical or horizontal edges, and is used to remove unwanted portions of a picture. You can crop any selected picture by clicking the **Picture Tools**, **Format**, **Size**, **Crop** button shown above.

Then do one of the following:

* To crop one side, drag the centre cropping handle on that side inward.

* To crop two adjacent sides at once, drag a corner handle inwards.

Fig. 6.20 Dragging the Top Left Cropping Handle

* To crop equally on two opposite sides at once, press and hold the Ctrl key while you drag the centre cropping handle on either side inward.

* To crop equally on all four sides at once, press and hold the Ctrl key and drag a corner cropping handle inward.

In the same **Size** group, the **Shape Height** and **Shape Width** buttons let you set exact dimensions for a selected picture.

Inserting Clip Art

Word 2007 has been given much more power in the finding, organising and displaying of graphic images such as photographs and clip art.

When you click the **Insert**, **Illustrations**, **Clip Art** button to import a graphic into a document, Word now opens the Clip Art task pane, as shown in Fig. 6.21.

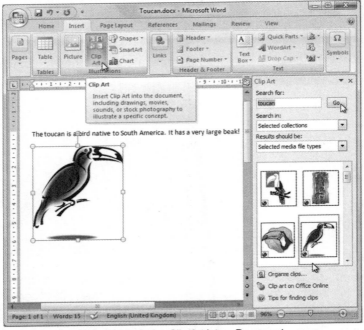

Fig. 6.21 Inserting Clip Art into a Document

This pane works in conjunction with the new Clip Organizer, as we shall soon see. Before we look at that though, type the word 'toucan' into the **Search for** box, and select **Microsoft Office Online** in the **Search in** box. Then, clicking the **Go** button should find over 20 drawings of the unusual South American bird for you to download and use in your documents. Just click the one you want in the task pane and it will be placed in your document, as above.

As clip art is just a type of graphic, it is not surprising that you use all the methods described in the previous pages to manipulate and format the pictures.

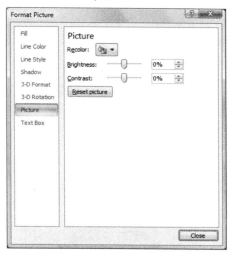

Fig. 6.22 The Format Picture Dialogue Box

Pointing to a graphic and right-clicking it displays a shortcut menu, the **Format Picture** option of which opens the Format Picture dialogue box, shown in Fig. 6.22 above. This gives you yet another way of changing and enhancing your pictures. We suggest you play around with these settings until you are happy with them.

The Clip Organizer

As we saw earlier, the Clip Art task pane lets you search for clip art, photos and other media files on keywords and titles. The search can be restricted to any of your disc drives or folders, or can include on-line sites on the Internet.

The Clip Organizer can help you organise your media files into separate collections on your hard disc so that you can easily find them later. The first time you open the Clip

Organizer, by clicking the **Organize clips** link in the Clip Art pane, you can choose to let it scan your computer for photos and other media files. It does not actually copy or move the files but creates shortcuts to them in collection folders. To re-catalogue your media, open the Clip Organizer and use the **File, Add Clips to Organizer**, **Automatically** command.

Fig. 6.23 The Clip Organizer Window

Once it has done this an Explorer type window opens up like ours in Fig. 6.23 above. If all is well, every graphic image on your computer will be listed in different folders under the 'My Collections' entry in the Collection List, which uses the left pane of the window. The Clip Organizer places your images in sub-folders that reflect the name of the folder in which they were found on the scanned disc. As you select a folder in this list its contents are shown as thumbnail images in the right pane.

Organising Your Pictures

After the Clip Organizer has scanned your computer the data it forms from your hard disc(s) will almost certainly need organising.

In our case over half the folders it created needed deleting, (right-click and select **Delete collection**), and more sensible keywords needed adding to the pictures that were kept. This is best done by right-clicking an image in the right pane and selecting **Preview/Properties** from the context menu.

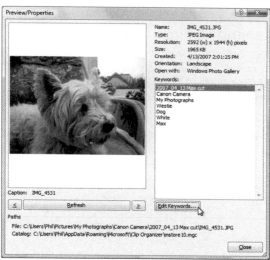

Fig. 6.24 The Preview/Properties Box

Fig. 6.24 shows the dialogue box that opens, in which you can name a picture by typing a **Caption**. Clicking the **Edit Keywords** button lets you add or delete keywords for the picture. These will help you when you search for particular images.

For more assistance, you can always press **F1**, or use the **Help**, **Clip Organizer Help** command, as the Organizer has its own Help System which is much easier to use than that for Word 2007.

Drawing in Word with Shapes

In Word a drawing is a drawing 'object', or a group of drawing objects on a canvas, including shapes, diagrams, flowcharts, curves, lines, and WordArt.

The Drawing Canvas

When you insert a drawing object in Word, it can be placed on a drawing canvas. Anything placed onto a drawing canvas is 'separated' from the background document. When you move the canvas, everything on it moves together.

To create a drawing in your document, click the **Insert**, **Illustrations**, **Shapes** button, and then click **New Drawing Canvas**. This places a new drawing canvas at the insertion point, as shown in Fig. 6.25 below.

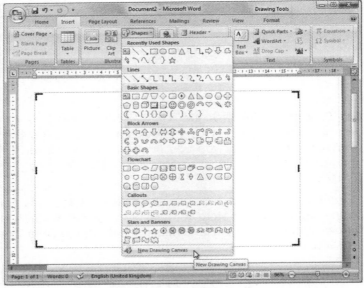

Fig. 6.25 Inserting a New Drawing Canvas

The canvas helps you arrange the drawings in the document. When first placed, a drawing canvas has no background or border, but you can control these and many other features by selecting it and using the Ribbon tools.

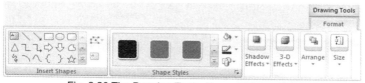

Fig. 6.26 The Drawing Tools, Format Ribbon Tab

The **Drawing Tools**, **Format** tab, shown above, is opened whenever a drawing canvas or shape is selected in your document.

Creating a Drawing

A drawing is usually made up of a group of objects, with each object being a constituent part of the drawing.

Fig. 6.27 The Insert Shapes More Button

To create an object on a drawing canvas, click the **Drawing Tools**, **Format**, **Insert Shapes**, **More** button, pointed to in Fig. 6.27. This will open the drop-down menu of the shapes available, as shown in Fig. 6.28 on the next page.

Select a shape that suits your needs, position the mouse pointer where you want to create the object on the drawing canvas, and then drag the mouse to draw the object. Hold the **Shift** key while you drag the mouse to lock the aspect ratio. For example, to create a circle, select the **Oval** shape and drag the pointer with the **Shift** key depressed. If you do not hold **Shift**, Word creates an oval. All the other shapes work in the same way.

If you want to draw freehand on the canvas, click the **Freeform** or **Scribble** tools in the **Lines** section above, and draw with the pointer. To stop drawing with these tools, just double-click.

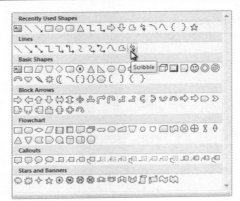

Fig. 6.28 The Drawing Shapes available in Word 2007

Editing a Drawing

To select an object, click on it. Word displays coloured handles around the object selected. To select multiple objects, hold the **Ctrl** key and click each one in turn. Shapes can then be re-sized, rotated, flipped, coloured, and combined to make more complex shapes. Some Shapes have a yellow adjustment handle that you can use to change the most prominent feature of a shape.

You can move an object, or multiple objects, within the canvas by selecting them and dragging to the desired position. To size an object, position the mouse pointer on one of its blue handles and then drag the handle until the object is the shape and size you want. To rotate an object, drag the green rotate handle.

To delete an object, select it and press the **Del** key. To delete a drawing, just delete the canvas.

To apply a style to a shape, rest the pointer over a style in the **Drawing Tools**, **Format**, **Shape Styles** group, to see a preview. Click the style to apply it. You can also click the **Shape Fill** or **Shape Outline** buttons (Fig. 6.29) and select the options that you want, or use shadow and 3-D effects to add more interest to your drawing shapes.

Fig. 6.29 Shape Styles and Shadow and 3-D Effects Groups

To align objects on the canvas, press and hold the **Ctrl** key while you select the objects that you want to align. In the **Arrange** group, click **Align** to choose from an assortment of alignment commands.

To adjust the size of the drawing canvas, select it and then click the arrows in the **Size** group, or click the **Size** Dialogue Box Launcher to make more precise adjustments.

Once you are happy with your drawing you can use the **Drawing Tools**, **Format**, **Arrange**, **Text Wrapping** button shown in Fig. 6.30. By default a canvas is placed **In Line With Text** and will only move with the text around it.

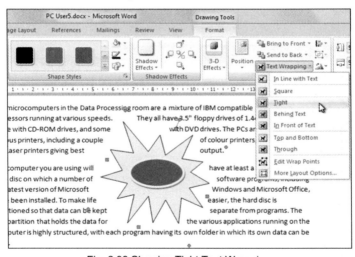

Fig. 6.30 Showing Tight Text Wrapping

In Fig. 6.30 we selected **Tight** wrapping and dragged the canvas to where we wanted it. As can be seen, the surrounding text wraps tightly over the canvas. Do try out some of these effects, they really are fun.

SmartArt Graphics

When you want to illustrate a process, or the relationship between hierarchical elements, you can create a dynamic, visually appealing diagram in Word 2007 using SmartArt Graphics. Using predefined sets of formatting, you can easily create the following diagrams:

Process   Visually describe the ordered set of steps required to complete a task.

Hierarchy   Illustrate the structure of an organisation.

Cycle   Represent a circular sequence of steps, tasks, or events; or the relationship of a set of steps, tasks, or events to a central, core element.

Relationship   Show convergent, divergent, overlapping, or merging, elements.

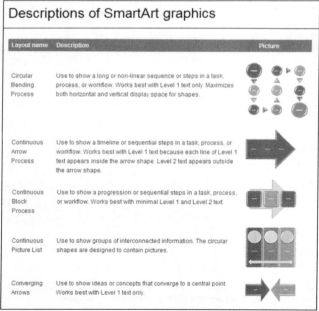

Fig. 6.31 Some of the Many SmartArt Graphics Layouts

To create a SmartArt graphic, click the **Insert**, **Illustrations**, **SmartArt** button, and select a style from the gallery as we show below.

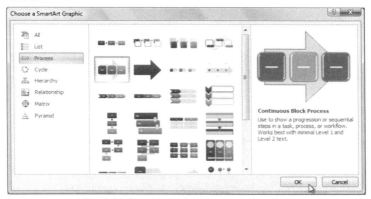

Fig. 6.32 Choosing a SmartArt Graphic Style

If you need help, just click the **Help** button ⓘ. We liked the **Continuous Block Process** option, so selected it and clicked the **OK** button.

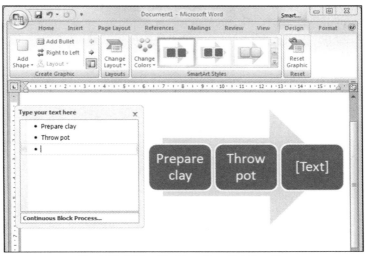

Fig. 6.33 Adding Text to a SmartArt Graphic

The SmartArt template is placed at the insertion point in your document, as shown in Fig. 6.33, ready for you to add text. You can just type the text into each element of the graphic, but we prefer to use the text box as shown. This is opened by clicking the button shown here, which is located on the left side of the graphic.

Once the SmartArt graphic is created you can move it, re-size it, rotate it, add more text to it, apply a different Quick Style to it, and make other changes, as you can with all the graphics.

This really is a very easy process, and the results can be excellent. It is well worth exploring in detail.

Inserting Objects into a Document

You can insert 'Objects' into a Word 2007 document to include information created in other Office programs or in many other Windows programs. An Object can take the form of a table, chart, graphic, equation, or other type of information. (In case you wondered, Objects created in one application, for example spreadsheets, and linked or embedded in another application are called OLE Objects.)

To insert an Object into a document use the **Insert**, **Text**, **Object** button 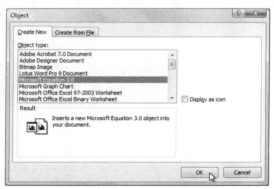, which opens the Object dialogue box.

Fig. 6.34 Creating a New Object

From this, you can choose different 'Object types', from say an Adobe Acrobat or a WordPro Document. Word may take several seconds to open this box as it scans your system to build the list of Object types you can use, depending on the software that you have installed.

For example, if you select 'Microsoft Equation 3.0' from the **Object type** list, as shown in Fig. 6.34, Word opens an old version of Equation Editor which allows you to build mathematical equations in your Word document. We presume this has been kept for backward compatibility, as Word 2007 has a new Equation Editor.

Inserting an Equation

If building equations is not your cup of tea, you can safely skip this section. If, on the other hand, you want to learn how to build equations, click the arrow next to the **Insert**, **Symbols**, **Equation** button and then either select a **Built-In** equation from the gallery, shown in Fig. 6.35, or click **Insert New Equation** to create one of your own.

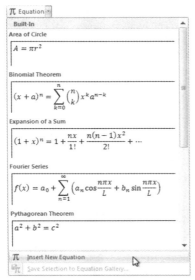

Fig. 6.35 The Equation Gallery

When you type an equation, it is automatically converted into a professionally formatted equation. When you open a document that contains an equation written in a previous version of Word, you cannot use the built-in support for writing and changing equations unless you convert your document to Word 2007. To do this, click the Microsoft Office button, and then click **Convert**.

An equation box is placed at the insertion point in the document and the **Equation Tools**, **Design** tab is opened on the Ribbon, as shown in Fig. 6.36.

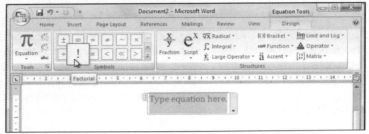

Fig. 6.36 The Equation Tools

We suggest you first press **F1** to display the Help window and search for Equation Editor, as shown in Fig. 6.37.

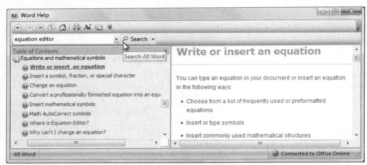

Fig. 6.37 Equation Help

In the **Equation Tools**, **Design**, **Structures** group, click the structure type that you want, and then select from the gallery that opens. This way you can insert templates that contain such structures as Fractions, Scripts, Radicals, Integrals, Operators, Brackets, Functions, Accents, Limit and Log functions and Matrices (Fig. 6.38). Templates can be nested, by inserting them in the slots of other templates, to build complex hierarchical formulas.

Fig. 6.38

If the structure contains placeholders, or dotted boxes as shown here, you click in them and when they turn blue you type the numbers or select symbols that you want.

The **Equation Tools**, **Design**, **Symbols** group has buttons for inserting hundreds of mathematical and other symbols, many of which are not available in the Symbol dialogue box described on page 107. To insert a symbol in an equation, click a symbol in the gallery, or click the **More** button and then select a specific symbol from the galleries that appear under the button.

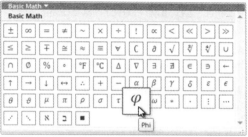

Fig. 6.39 The Basic Math Symbols Gallery

Fig. 6.40

There are eight groups of symbols available, which can be selected from the drop-down menu that opens when you click the down-arrow shown here in Fig. 6.40.

As an example, we will take you through the steps required, when using the Equation Editor, to construct the equation for the solution of a quadratic equation, as shown here.

$$x = \frac{-b \pm \sqrt{\{b^2 - 4ac\}}}{2a}$$

This is actually one of the **Built-In** equation options available to you, but we will use it as an example.

$$x = \frac{-b \pm \sqrt{\{b^2 - 4ac\}}}{2a}$$

To construct this equation, place the insertion pointer at the required place in your document, click the **Insert**, **Symbols**, **Equation** button to open the Equation Editor, and follow the steps listed below.

- Type **x =** followed by the **Stacked Fraction** template $\frac{\square}{\square}$ from the **Structures** group.

- Select the top placeholder and type **-b** followed by the $\pm$ symbol from the **Symbols** group.

- Select the **Square Root** template $\sqrt{\square}$ from the **Structures**, **Radical** gallery.

- In the placeholder, select the **Brackets** template $\{\square\}$ from the **Structures**, **Bracket** gallery.

- Select the **Superscript** template $\square^{\square}$ from the **Structures**, **Script** gallery and type **b** in the bottom slot and **2** in the top one. Re-position the insertion pointer as shown here $\sqrt{\{b^2\}}$, and then type **-4ac**.

- Position the insertion pointer in the denominator placeholder and type **2a**. That's all there is to it.

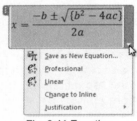

Fig. 6.41 Equation Options

When you are happy with your equation, you can click the **Equation Options** button, shown here. On this menu, the **Linear** option converts the equation so it is all on one line, the **Professional** option converts it back again, and **Change to Inline** sets the equation to flow with the surrounding text.

To add an equation to the **Built-In** equation list, you use the **Save as New Equation** option. In the Create New Building Block dialogue box, type a name for the equation, and in the **Gallery** list, click **Equations**. This example should get you started with equations. Try it, it's simpler than it looks.

Building Blocks

Building Blocks are reusable document parts, or content, that are stored in galleries. You can use them at any time, or save a selection to create a new building block.

Using a Building Block

To use a Building Block, click the pointer where you want to insert it in your document, click the **Insert**, **Text**, **Quick Parts** button (Fig. 6.42), and then select **Building Blocks Organizer**. This opens the window shown in Fig. 6.43 below. You can click **Name** to sort the listing by name, or **Gallery** to sort by Gallery. Make your choice and click **Insert**.

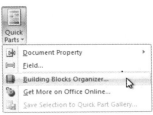

Fig. 6.42 Quick Parts Menu

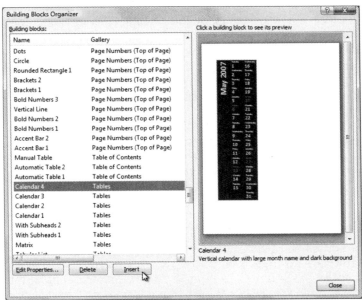

Fig. 6.43 The Building Blocks Organizer

Saving a Building Block

As we saw at the end of the Equations section, you can add your own Building Blocks to any of the galleries available in Word 2007. To do this, select the text or graphic that you want to store as a reusable building block, click the **Insert**, **Text**, **Quick Parts** button and select the **Save Selection to Quick Part Gallery** to open the box below.

Fig. 6.44 Creating a New Building Block

Fill out the information in the Create New Building Block dialogue box. Type a unique name for the building block in the **Name** text box, and select the gallery that you want the building block to be in, in the **Gallery** text box. The other information boxes are not important, but may help you later. Clicking the **OK** button will save the block.

Note: Perhaps the most useful built-in Building Blocks are the cover pages that can be used as opening pages for your documents. These are well worth some exploration.

7

Using Tables and Charts

The ability to use 'Tables' is built into most top-range word processors these days. At first glance the process might look complicated and perhaps only a small percentage of users take advantage of the facility, which is a pity because using a Table has many possibilities. If you have worked with a spreadsheet, such as Excel or Lotus 1-2-3, then you are familiar with the principle of tables.

Tables are used to create adjacent columns of text and numeric data. A table is simply a grid of columns and rows with the intersection of a column and row forming a rectangular box which is referred to as a 'cell'. In Word you can include pictures, charts, notes, footnotes, tabs, other tables and page breaks in your tables. There are several ways to place information into a table:

- Type the desired text, or numeric data.

- Paste text from the main document.

- Link two tables within a document.

- Insert data created in another application.

- Import a picture.

- Create a chart on information held in a table.

The data is placed into individual cells that are organised into columns and rows, similar to a spreadsheet. You can modify the appearance of table data by applying text formatting and enhancements, or by using different styles.

Creating a Table

Tables can be created by clicking the **Insert**, **Tables**, **Table** button and selecting **Insert Table**. Using this method, displays the dialogue box shown in Fig. 7.1, which lets you size the column widths at that point.

As an example we will step through the process of creating the table shown in Fig. 7.5 on page 145. Open a 'New' file (it could be an existing file, in which case you place the insertion point where you want the table to appear), then click on the **Insert**, **Tables**, **Table** button and drag down and to the right.

Fig. 7.1 Inserting a Table

As you drag the mouse, the selection expands to create a grid of rows and columns, as shown in Fig. 7.2. At the top of the box is an automatic display of the number of rows and columns you are currently selecting. When you release the mouse button, a table is inserted in your document the size of the selected grid.

Fig. 7.2 Using The Table Button

For our example, we require an 11 x 4 table with 11 rows and 4 columns of cells, but as the maximum number of rows available on this quick grid is 8, accept 8 x 4. Once this appears in position in the document, the cursor is placed in the top left cell awaiting your input. The cells forming the table are displayed with lines around each cell, as shown in Fig. 7.3 on the next page.

As you should expect by now with Word 2007, a Table Tools tab is opened whenever a table is selected in a document. This gives you access to two extra tabs to **Design** and **Format** your tables, as shown in Fig. 7.3.

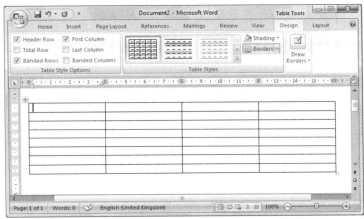

Fig. 7.3 A New Table and Table Tools Design Tab

To add extra rows to your table, just select a cell and click the **Table Tools**, **Layout**, **Rows & Columns**, **Insert Below** button, pointed to below.

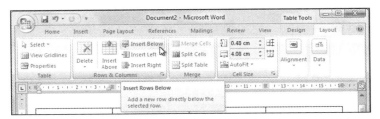

Fig. 7.4 Inserting Rows from the Table Tools Layout Tab

To move around in a table, simply click the desired cell to select it, or use one of the keyboard commands listed on the next page.

Navigating with the Keyboard

To navigate around a table when using the keyboard, use the following keys:

Press this	*To do this*
Tab	Moves the insertion point right one cell, in the same row, and from the last cell in one row to the first cell in the next row. If the cell contains information it highlights the contents.
Shift+Tab	Moves the insertion point left one cell. If the cell contains information it highlights the contents.
↑,↓,←, and →	Moves the insertion point within cells, between cells, and between the cells in a table and the main document text.
Home	Moves the insertion point to the beginning of the current line within a cell.
Alt+Home	Moves the insertion point to the first column in the current row.
End	Moves the insertion point to the end of the current line within a cell.
Alt+End	Moves the insertion point to the last column in the current row.
Alt+PgUp	Moves the insertion point to the top cell in the column.
Alt+PgDn	Moves the insertion point to the bottom cell in the column.

Now type in the information given below and format your table using the **Home**, **Paragraph** buttons on the Ribbon to align the contents of the various cells as shown.

Fruit Purchases			
Type of Fruit	**Cost (£/kg)**	**Weight (kg)**	**Amount (£)**
Cox apples	1.89	5.6	
Conference pears	1.00	11.6	
Oranges	0.60	23.2	
Bananas	1.20	8.5	
Physalis	7.90	1.8	
		Total	

Fig. 7.5 Our Example Table

To enter the heading as shown, move the pointer to the left of the top row and when it changes to a

Fig. 7.6 The
Borders Button

🖱 shape, drag it to the right to highlight all the cells of the first row. Then click the **Table Tools**, **Layout**, **Merge**, **Merge Cells** button to join all the cells into one. Now you can type the heading, centre it (**Ctrl+E** is the easiest way), format it in bold, and increase its font size to your liking.

The line in the cell of the penultimate row and last column was entered by selecting the cell, clicking the down-arrow of the **Table Tools**, **Design**, **Table Styles**, **Borders** button and selecting **Horizontal Line** from the menu, as shown here in Fig. 7.6.

The other options in this drop-down menu give you complete control over what cell and table border lines will be displayed in your document. Being able to display a table without border lines means you can use it to format column type data in a document without having to resort to tabs and tab settings.

Changing Column Width and Row Height

The column width of selected cells or entire columns can be changed by dragging the table column markers on the ruler or by dragging the column boundaries, as shown in Fig. 7.7.

Type of Fruit	←‖→ Cost (£/kg)

Fig. 7.7 Changing Column Width

You can also drag a column boundary while holding down certain keys. The overall effects of these actions being:

Key used	*Effect*
No key	Only the columns to the left and right are re-sized proportionally with the overall width of the table remaining the same size.
Shift key	Only the column to the left is re-sized with the overall width of the table changing by the same amount.
Ctrl key	As the column to the left changes, all columns to the right change proportionally, but the overall width of the table remains the same.

The height of a row depends on its contents. As you type text into a cell, its height increases to accommodate it. You can increase the height of a cell by inserting empty lines before or after the text by pressing the **Enter** key. All other cells in that row become the same height as the largest cell. You can also increase the height of rows by dragging a row boundary up or down, as shown in Fig. 7.8.

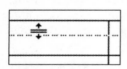

Fig. 7.8 Changing Row Height

Cell dimensions can also be changed by right-clicking in the table and using the **Table Properties** command to display a dialogue box with tabs for controlling size and the placement of a table, the column and row size, as well as the vertical alignment of entries within cells.

When you have finished, save your work so far under the filename **Table 1**. We will use this table to show you how you can insert expressions into cells to make your table behave just like a spreadsheet.

Entering Expressions

To enter an expression into a table cell, so that you can carry out spreadsheet type calculations, select the cell and click the **Table Tools**, **Layout**, **Data**, **Formula** button which opens the dialogue box shown below. Word automatically analyses the table and suggests an appropriate formula in the Formula box of the displayed dialogue box, as shown in Fig. 7.9.

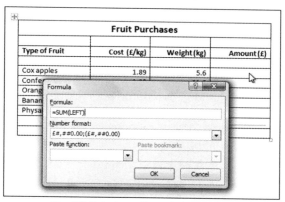

Fig. 7.9 Entering a Formula into a Cell

In the above situation, it has found numbers in cells to the left of the highlighted cell (D5 pointed to above), therefore it suggests the SUM(LEFT) formula. To replace this formula, simply delete it from the **Formula** box and type the new formula preceded by the equal (=) sign.

For example, to calculate the cost of apples purchased in Sterling (£) in cell D5, type the following formula in the **Formula** box:

```
=B5*C5
```

Word performs mathematical calculations on numbers in cells and inserts the result of the calculation as a field in the cell that contains the insertion pointer. Cells are referred to as A1, A2, B1, B2, and so on, with the letter representing a column and the number representing a row. Thus, B3 refers to the hatched cell.

	A	B	C
1			
2			
3		▨	

When you use the **Table Tools**, **Layout**, **Data**, **Formula** command, Word assumes addition, unless you indicate otherwise, and proposes a sum based on the following rules:

- If the cell that contains the insertion pointer is at the intersection of a row and column and both contain numbers, Word sums the column. To sum the row, type =SUM(LEFT) or =SUM(RIGHT) in the **Formula** box, depending on the location of the insertion pointer.

- If the cell that contains the insertion pointer contains text or numbers, they are ignored.

- Word evaluates numbers beginning with the cell closest to the cell that contains the insertion pointer and continues until it reaches either a blank cell or a cell that contains text.

- If the numbers you are calculating include a number format, such as a £ sign, the result will also contain that format.

Fill in the rest of column D (unfortunately you will have to retype the formula in each cell as there is no apparent method of replication), then to calculate the total cost, place the insertion pointer in cell D11 and click the **Table Tools**, **Layout**, **Data**, **Formula** button. Word analyses your table and suggests the following function:

```
=SUM(ABOVE)
```

which is the correct formula in this case. When you press **OK**, Word calculates the result and places it in cell D11, as shown on the following page. Save your work again for future use, but this time with the filename **Table 2**.

Fruit Purchases			
Type of Fruit	**Cost (£/kg)**	**Weight (kg)**	**Amount (£)**
Cox apples	1.89	5.60	£ 10.58
Conference pears	1.00	11.60	£ 11.60
Oranges	0.60	23.20	£ 13.92
Bananas	1.20	8.50	£ 10.20
Physalis	7.90	1.80	£ 14.22
		Total	£ 60.52

Fig. 7.10 Example Table with Calculated Cells

As the result of a calculation is inserted as a field in the cell that contains the insertion pointer, if you change the contents of the referenced cells, you must update the calculation. To do this, select the field (the cell that contains the formula) by highlighting it and press the **F9** function key.

In a formula you can specify any combination of mathematical and logical operators from the following list.

Addition	+
Subtraction	−
Multiplication	*
Division	/
Percent	%
Powers and roots	^
Equal to	=
Less than	<
Less than or equal to	<=
Greater than	>
Greater than or equal to	>=
Not equal to	< >

The functions below accept references to table cells:

ABS( )	AND( )	AVERAGE( )
COUNT( )	DEFINED( )	FALSE( )
IF( )	INT( )	MAX( )
MIN( )	MOD( )	NOT( )
OR( )	PRODUCT( )	ROUND( )
SIGN( )	SUM( )	TRUE( )

The main reason for using formulas in a table, instead of just typing in the numbers, is that formulas will still give the correct final answer even if some of the data is changed.

If you change any cells referenced in a calculation, you can update the calculation by selecting the field and then pressing **F9**. As Word table calculations have to be manually recalculated like this, it is usually better to insert a Microsoft Excel spreadsheet table, to perform more complex calculations. This is done by clicking the **Insert**, **Tables**, **Table** button and selecting **Excel Spreadsheet** (see Fig. 7.2). A small sheet is placed at the insertion point which uses all the facilities of Excel 2007.

If you need help with Excel then may we suggest you keep a lookout for *Microsoft Excel 2007 explained* and *Microsoft Office 2007 explained*, both published by BERNARD BABANI (publishing) Ltd.

Editing a Table

You can edit a table by inserting or deleting columns or rows, or by merging or splitting cells, as follows:

To insert a column or row: Select the cell where you want the new row or column to appear, then click one of the **Table Tools**, **Layout**, **Rows & Columns** group buttons shown here. This version of Word allows you to insert columns or rows to either side of the selected cell, as well as single cells.

Fig. 7.11 the
Delete Button

To delete a cell, a column or row: Select the cell whose column or row you want to delete, click the **Table Tools**, **Layout**, **Rows & Columns**, **Delete** button, and choose an option from the drop-down menu shown in Fig. 7.11. As you can see from the available options, you can even delete a single cell or an entire table.

To merge cells: Select the cells you want to merge, then click the **Table Tools**, **Layout**, **Merge**, **Merge Cells** button shown here.

To split cells: Move the insertion pointer to the cell you want to split, then click the **Table Tools**, **Layout**, **Merge**, **Split Cells** button. The dialogue box shown in Fig. 7.12 is displayed which can be used to subdivide a cell.

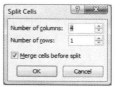

Fig. 7.12 Split Cells

To split a table: To split a table, click the row that you want to be the first row of the second table and click the **Table Tools**, **Layout**, **Merge**, **Split Table** button. Using this command on the first row of a table, allows you to insert text before a table. In Fig. 7.13, the insertion pointer was placed in the second row and the table was split.

Fruit Purchases			
Type of Fruit	Cost (£/kg)	Weight (kg)	Amount (£)
Cox apples	1.89	5.60	10.58
Conference pears	1.00	11.60	11.60
Oranges	0.60	23.20	13.92
Bananas	1.20	8.50	10.20
Physalis	7.90	1.80	14.22
		Total	£ 60.52

Fig. 7.13 Splitting a Table into Two

To align cell content: Select the cells you want to align, then click the **Table Tools**, **Layout**, **Alignment** group buttons shown here. You can set all 9 combinations of vertical and horizontal alignment with the left-hand buttons. Clicking the **Text Direction** button repeatedly, steps through text pointing to the right, pointing down and pointing up. The **Cell Margins** button opens the Table Options box where you can control cell margins and spacings.

Formatting a Table

You can enhance the looks of a table by selecting one of many pre-defined styles. As an example, open the previously saved version of **Table 2**, place the insertion pointer in a table cell and move through the options in the **Table Tools**, **Design**, **Table Styles** gallery, as shown below.

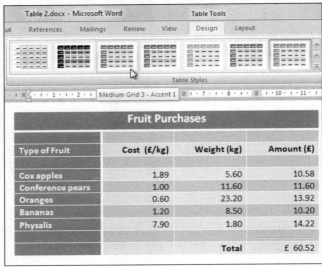

Fig. 7.14 Adding a Built-in Style to a Table

We selected 'Medium Grid 3 Accent 1' from the **Table Styles** gallery, as shown in Fig. 7.14, to produce a very professional looking table.

Finally, save the result of this formatting as **Table 3**.

Using Charts or Graphs

Word 2007 makes it easy to create professional looking charts or graphs from your data. The saying 'a picture is worth a thousand words', applies equally well to charts and figures. They allow you to visually see data trends and patterns right there in your document.

As long as you have Excel 2007 installed, you can create Excel charts in Word. They are embedded in Word, and the chart data is stored in an Excel worksheet that is incorporated in the Word file.

If Excel 2007 is not installed when you create a new chart in Word 2007, Microsoft Graph opens. A chart then appears with its associated data in a table called a datasheet. You can enter your own data in the datasheet, import data from a text file to the datasheet, or paste data from another program to the datasheet.

Adding a Graph or Chart

In Word, click where you want to insert the chart, and click the **Insert**, **Illustrations**, **Chart** button ![Chart]. In the Insert Chart dialogue box, select a chart type, and then click OK.

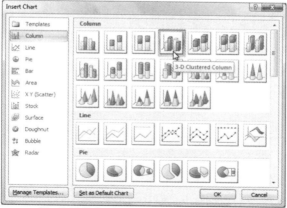

Fig. 7.15 Selecting the Type of Chart to Add

A sample chart of the type selected is placed in your document, as shown in Fig. 7.16 below.

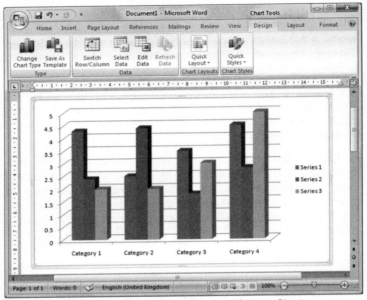

Fig. 7.16 The Sample 3-D Clustered Column Chart

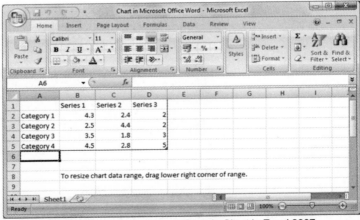

Fig. 7.17 Data for the Above Sample Chart in Excel 2007

As shown in Fig. 7.17, Excel 2007 opens in its own window and displays the sample data for the chart on a worksheet.

To create your own chart you have to replace the sample data in Excel by clicking a cell on the worksheet and then typing the data that you want. You also need to replace the sample axis labels in Column A and the legend entry names in Row 1, as we have done in Fig. 7.18.

	A	B	C	D	E
1		Cost (£/kg)	Weight (kg)	Amount (£)	
2	Apples	1.89	5.6	10.58	
3	Pears	1.00	11.6	11.60	
4	Oranges	0.60	23.2	13.92	
5	Bananas	1.20	8.5	10.20	
6	Physalis	7.90	1.8	14.22	
7					
8		To resize chart data range, drag lower right corner of range.			

Fig. 7.18 Our Edited Data in Excel 2007

After you update the worksheet, the chart in Word is updated automatically with the new data, and three tabs of **Chart Tools** are added to the Word Ribbon.

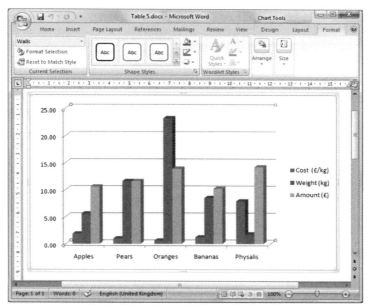

Fig. 7.19 The Charted Data in Word 2007

When you have finished editing your data, you need to save it in Excel, by clicking the **Office Button**, and using **Save As**, but make sure you give it a new name. You can then close Excel.

Pre-defined Chart Types

To select a different type of chart, click the **Chart Tools**, **Design**, **Type**, **Change Chart Type** button shown here. There are 11 basic chart types, and with variations there are 73 type options in all. These chart-types are normally used to describe the following relationships between data:

Area: for showing a volume relationship between two series, such as production or sales, over a given length of time.

Bar: for comparing differences in data (noncontinuous data that are not related over time) by depicting changes in horizontal bars to show positive and negative variations from a given position.

Bubble: for showing a type of XY (scatter) chart. The size of the data (radius of the bubble) indicates the value of a third variable.

Column: for comparing separate items (noncontinuous data which are related over time) by depicting changes in vertical bars to show positive and negative variations from a given position.

Doughnut: for comparing parts with the whole. Similar to pie charts, but can depict more than one series of data.

Line: for showing continuous changes in data with time.

Pie: for comparing parts with the whole. You can use this type of chart when you want to compare the percentage of an item from a single series of data with the whole series.

Radar: for plotting one series of data as angle values defined in radians, against one or more series defined in terms of a radius.

Surface: for showing optimum combinations between two sets of data, as in a topographic map. Colours and patterns indicate areas that are in the same range of values.

Stock: for showing high-low-close type of data variation to illustrate stock market prices or temperature changes.

XY (Scatter):   for showing scatter relationships between X and Y. Scatter charts are used to depict items which are not related over time.

The Chart Tools

When you select a chart in Word by clicking it, the **Chart Tools** add the **Design**, **Layout**, and **Format** tabs, as below.

Fig. 7.20 The Design Tab of the Chart Tools

The Design tab groups controls for you to change the Chart Type, Data, Chart Layouts, Chart Styles and Location.

Fig. 7.21 The Layout Tab of the Chart Tools

With the Layout tab you control the layout of the Current Selection, Labels, and Axes, Insert a layout, and Background, Analysis and Properties.

Fig. 7.22 The Format Tab of the Chart Tools

From the Format tab you can format the Current Selection, set Shape Styles and WordArt Styles, Arrange objects and Size.

When you click outside the graph area, the chart is embedded in your Word document. To move it, as with all of Word's graphics, select the graph, click the **Page Layout**, **Arrange**, **Text Wrapping** button and select a wrapping style such as **Tight**, as shown earlier in Fig. 6.16. The default setting is **In Line with Text**. Once this is done you can simply drag the graph wherever you want in your document.

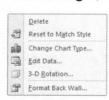

Fig. 7.23 Chart Context Menu

To edit the data for a chart, right-click the chart area and select **Edit Data** from the context menu shown in Fig. 7.23. This opens the Excel worksheet as shown in Fig. 7.18.

Customising a Chart

Now it is time for you to 'play'. The only way to find out what all the charting controls do is to try them all out. Remember that some options are applied to the chart element that is currently selected, others to the whole chart.

Fig. 7.24 The Chart Elements Box

To control what is selected, click the arrow next to the **Chart Elements** box in the **Current Selection** group of the **Format** tab, and then click the chart element that you want.

On the **Layout** tab, we suggest you click the label layout option that you want in the **Labels** group, select what chart axes you want in the **Axes** group, and what layout option you want in the **Background** group.

In the **Current Selection** group, clicking **Format Selection**, opens a Format control box like that shown in Fig. 7.25, in which you select the formatting options you want for the selected chart element.

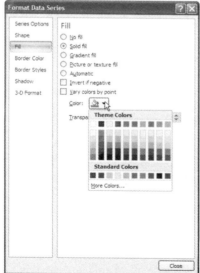

Fig. 7.25 Setting Format Options for Chart Elements

You can also apply a quick style to individual elements, or use the **Shape Fill** , **Shape Outline** , and **Shape Effects** buttons in the **Shape Quick Styles** group on the **Format** tab. These are our favourite ways of formatting our charts.

Changing Titles and Labels

 To add or change a title, an axis label, or a legend within a chart you use the command buttons in the **Chart Tools**, **Layout**, **Labels** group shown here.

When you click them on the chart, you will see that these elements are individual objects (they are surrounded by small green circles and squares called 'handles') and you can edit, reposition, or change their font and point size. You can even rotate text within such areas in any direction you like.

When you have carried out all the improvements and changes to your chart, save the Word document as **Table 4**.

We are sure that you will get many hours of fun with the various Chart features and, more to the point, produce some very professional graphics for your reports. Good luck.

8

Managing Your Documents

If you need to work with large documents, or documents split into multiple files (such as the chapters of a book), you may be interested in knowing something about Word's Outline view, and other ways of managing your documents.

Outline View

Outline View provides a special way of looking at and organising the structure of a document. Ten outline levels can be used and these can automatically be based on the default Word styles (if they are used in your document), or on 'Levels' that you set yourself (Level 1 through to Level 9, plus Body text).

The following display shows part of the first page of Chapter 1 of this book in the normal Print Layout view.

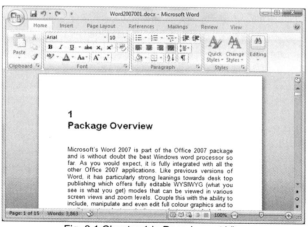

Fig. 8.1 Chapter 1 in Page Layout View

The same chapter is shown in Outline View in Fig. 8.2 below, obtained by either pressing the **Outline** button ▓ on the **Status Bar**, or by clicking the **View**, **Document Views**, **Outline** button on the Ribbon. In our case we have not used the default Word styles for the document so before seeing exactly what is shown here, we had to assign Outline Levels to the various Headings. This is easily done by selecting the heading and assigning a level to it using the **Outlining**, **Outline Tools**, **Outline Level** button on the Ribbon.

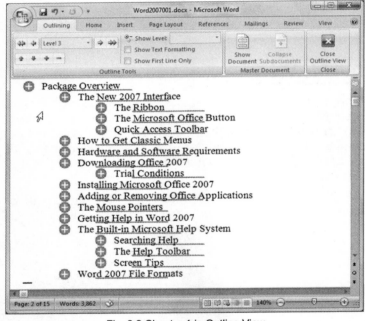

Fig. 8.2 Chapter 1 in Outline View

Once an outline like this has been created it is easy to move paragraphs around, to promote or demote them in the document ranking, or to delete them. Each operation includes all the subordinate paragraphs and text. Many writers use Outline view in this way to plan the framework of their project and when they are happy with it, they type the body text under the different headings in Print Layout view.

The Outline Tools

Fig. 8.3 The Outline Tools Group

The **Outline Tools** group, shown here, is on the **Outlining** tab which opens automatically when you change to Outline View mode. The functions of the buttons are:

Button	*Function*
	Promote to Heading 1 – Assigns heading to the top outline level.
	Promote – Assigns heading to the next higher outline level.
Level 1	**Outline Level** – The list of available levels. This is used to manually set outline levels to your document paragraphs.
	Demote – Assigns to the next lower outline level.
	Demote to Body Text – Assigns the active paragraph as body text.
	Move Up – Moves selected text before the paragraph preceding it.
	Move Down – Moves selected text after the paragraph following it.
	Expand – Displays hidden subordinate headings until text is reached.
	Collapse – Hides displayed subordinate text or lower level headings.
All Levels	**Show Level** – Displays all headings and text to the lowest selected level.

The actual formatting of the text can only be seen if the **Show Text Formatting** box is checked. In our Fig. 8.2, this box was not checked so the text appears in a standard font.

Using the expand and collapse buttons, you can display the entire document or only selected text. Editing a document in Outline mode is simple because you can control the level of detail that displays and quickly see the structure of the document. If you want to focus on the main topics in the document, you can collapse the text to display only paragraph styles set to high outline levels. If you want to view additional detail, you can expand the text to display text using paragraph styles set to lower outline levels.

Outline Symbols

Another feature of the outline view mode are the symbols placed before each paragraph (⊕ and ●). These not only show the status of the paragraph, but can be used to quickly manipulate paragraph text.

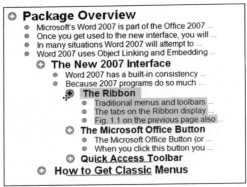

Fig. 8.4 Manipulating Paragraphs with the Outline Symbols

The ⊕ symbol is placed before paragraphs of Level 1 to 9, and the ● symbol is placed before Body Text. When you click a symbol, its level is shown in the **Outline Level** box on the Ribbon.

To display, or hide, subordinate text double-click a ⊕ button. Clicking on a symbol will select its subordinate text, as shown in Fig. 8.4. You can then drag it, to move the text to a new location in the document. Word automatically moves the text as you drag the mouse. When you drag a heading's symbol like this, the subheadings and body text under it also move or change levels. As you drag, Word displays a horizontal line at each heading level, as shown in Fig. 8.5 below.

Fig. 8.5 Dragging Paragraphs in an Outline

Releasing the mouse button will assign the text to that level. The corresponding heading level is applied to the heading.

An underline symbol under a heading indicates that the paragraph is collapsed and has hidden subordinate text or lower level headings. Double-clicking the ⊕ button will display these.

Closing Outline View

When you have finished outlining your document, click the **Outlining**, **Close**, **Close Outline View** button, shown here, to return you to the Print Layout view.

Creating a Table of Contents

Word 2007 makes it very easy to create a table of contents for an open document. This works especially well if you have used the heading styles – Heading 1, Heading 2, and Heading 3 – in the document. Word searches for headings that match your chosen styles, formats and indents the entry text according to the heading style, and then inserts the table of contents into the document.

To create a table of contents in Page Layout view, position the insertion point where you want the table of contents to appear. This will usually be at the beginning of the document. Next, click the **References**, **Table of Contents**, **Table of Contents** command button, and select the table of contents style that you want, as shown in Fig. 8.6.

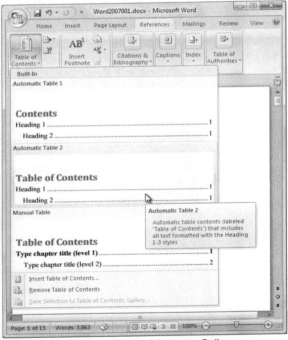

Fig. 8.6 The Table of Contents Gallery

For our sample chapter file this automatically created the table of contents shown in Fig. 8.7 below.

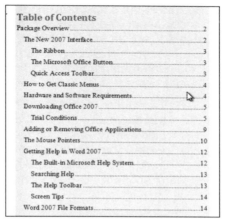

Fig. 8.7 The Table of Contents

For a long document this can save you quite a lot of time. Note that each line in the Table of Contents is now also a hyperlink to the corresponding heading in the document. To use these links you click the Table of Contents reference with the **Ctrl** key depressed.

If you add or remove headings or other table of contents entries in your document, you can quickly update the table of contents by clicking the **References**, **Table of Contents**, **Update Table** button and selecting to **Update page numbers only** or **Update entire table**.

To delete a table of contents click the **References**, **Table of Contents**, **Table of Contents**, and select **Remove Table of Contents**.

If you want the table of contents to include text that is not formatted as a heading, select the text, click the **References**, **Table of Contents**, **Add Text** button and choose the level for your selection. Repeat this procedure until you have labelled all of the text that you want to appear in the table of contents.

Creating an Index

An index, like the one at the back of this book, lists the main terms used in a document and shows the pages that they appear on. You can create an index manually, as we prefer, or let Word create it for you. This is not as easy as it sounds though, before you can create an index, you must first mark all the text you want to appear in it.

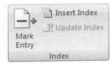

To do this, select a word or phrase in the document text that you want as an index entry and click the **References**, **Index**, **Mark Entry** ribbon button shown here, or more quickly, press the **Alt+Shift+X** keyboard shortcut, to open the box shown in Fig. 8.8 below.

Fig. 8.8 Marking Text to be Included in the Index

To create the main index entry, type or edit the text in the **Main entry** box. You can customise the entry by creating a **Subentry** or by creating a cross-reference to another entry.

Fig. 8.9 Inserted Index Code

When you click the **Mark** button an XE (Index Entry) field is added to your document, as shown here in Fig. 8.9.

Word also sets your document to show all formatting characters. You then work your way through the document marking all the entries you want. This can be quite a time consuming procedure, especially for a long document!

To create the index, click where you want to insert the finished index and use the tab **References**, **Index**, **Insert Index** button to open the following box.

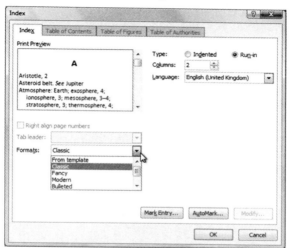

Fig. 8.10 Marking Text to be Included in the Index

Select an index design from the **Formats** box or design your own custom index layout and click the **OK** button.

To edit an index entry, find its XE field, in our case for example, { XE "Word" } and change the text inside the quotation marks. If you don't see the XE fields in your document, click the **Home**, **Paragraph**, **Show/Hide** button on the ribbon to display them.

To delete an index entry, select the entire index entry field, including the braces ({}), and then press the **Delete** key.

To update the index, click in it, and press **F9**, or click the **References**, **Index**, **Update Index** button.

Assembling a Master Document

If you are involved in writing long 'documents', such as books, it is sometimes best if you split them into chapters, each having its own file. Anything above 20 to 30 pages can get very unwieldy and, particularly if it contains graphics, may strain your computer's resources.

If you have broken your long document (book) into smaller files (chapters) you can work with these separately until you need to print your work in its entirety, or create a table of contents or index showing the whole document page numbers. You can then create a 'Master Document'.

One method of doing this is to open a new document in Word 2007, go into Outline View mode and type a document title. Next, on a new line press the **Outlining**, **Master Document**, **Insert Subdocument** button 📄Insert, then locate and select the file you want to insert into your Master Document from the Open dialogue box. This document is then inserted in your Master Document as shown in our example below.

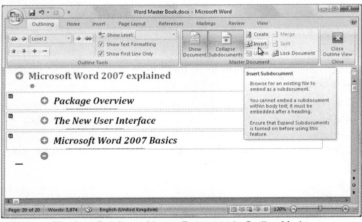

Fig. 8.11 Building a Master Document in Outline Mode

As can be seen in Fig. 8.11, the subdocument is placed in a 'section box' and a new 🖺 symbol is added to the outline.

You can drag this symbol around the outline screen to move the subdocument around the master document.

You can also add a new subdocument that does not have an existing file. To do this, place the insertion point on a new line of the master document and click the **Outlining**, **Master Document**, **Create Subdocument** button. Then type a heading for the subdocument. Use the **Outline Tools** buttons on the **Outlining** ribbon to promote or demote this entry to the same outline level as any other subdocument entries.

When you are finished you can save the master document from the **Office Button** 🏛 menu.

You can print the Master Document to paper in its entirety, by clicking the **Outlining**, **Master Document**, **Expand Subdocuments** button, then switching to Print Layout view and print as usual. We strongly recommend you use the **Print Preview** feature first, though.

We were very surprised that there seems to be no help on this feature available. Perhaps nobody uses it!

File Management

As we saw earlier in Chapter 3, you can carry out many of your document management functions from the **Open** and **Save As** dialogue boxes, accessed from the **Office Button** 🏛 menu. You do this by locating the folders or files you want to work with and using the right-click context menu options shown earlier in Fig. 3.35.

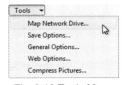

Fig. 8.12 Tools Menu

The **Tools** button provides additional options for working with files. A typical sub-menu of Tools options is shown here in Fig. 8.12. Some of these are also available on the context menus that open when you right-click a listed file.

Mapping Network Drives

The **Map Network Drive** option lets you easily access a folder located on a network by giving it a drive letter, as shown in Fig. 8.13 below.

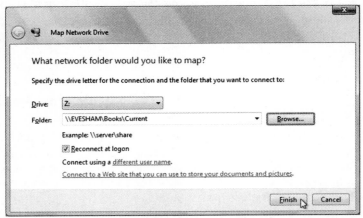

Fig. 8.13 Mapping a Network Drive

Here we are mapping a folder on one of our networked PCs as the **Z:** drive. We found the folder by clicking the **Browse** button and stepping through the folders in the network. Once the **Finish** button was clicked, we were able to access that folder as the Z: drive of the computer we were actually using.

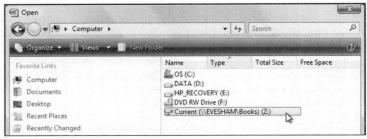

Fig. 8.14 Accessing a Mapped Drive from the Open Dialogue Box

This is shown in Fig. 8.14 above, which shows the network folder as drive Z: in the **Computer** window.

Compressing Pictures

As we have seen in an earlier chapter, Word 2007 is very good at handling graphic images in your documents. You can re-size and even edit them within Word itself. The only drawback to this is the enormous file sizes that can result.

With Word 2007, if you choose the **Save As** option and click the **Tools** button you will find the option to **Compress Pictures**, as shown in the menu in Fig. 8.12.

Clicking this opens the Compress Pictures box shown at the top in Fig. 8.15 below. Clicking the **Options** button opens the Compression Settings box.

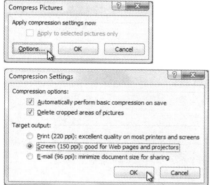

Fig. 8.15 Compress Pictures Settings

Here you can choose to compress all the pictures in the document and to delete any cropped areas (to reduce file size).

The **Print** option compresses to a resolution of 220 ppi, (pixels per inch) which is good enough for most print jobs. If you need to print at higher resolutions you should obviously **not** use these options.

The **Screen** option compresses pictures to a resolution of 150 ppi which is good for projectors and screen viewing.

The **E-mail** option compresses pictures to 96 ppi, which is really the minimum for clear screen viewing.

The Favorite Links Bar

Fig. 8.16 The Default Favorite Links Bar

The **Favorite Links** bar is at the left side in some dialogue boxes, such as **Save As**, **Open**, and **Insert Picture**. You can use it to quickly access commonly used folders where you want to store your files for easier access.

By default, the bar contains shortcuts to the **Documents**, **Computer**, **Desktop**, **Recent Places**, and **Recently Changed** folders, as shown here, but you can add your own links to the list.

The Links are actually kept in a folder of their own which you can open by right-clicking below the Favorite Links bar and selecting the **Open Favorite Links Folder** option.

To add a link to any folder to the bar you locate its icon or name in the Computer window and drag it with the right mouse button depressed into the Favorite Links folder.

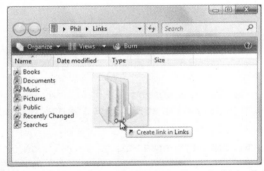

Fig. 8.17 Dragging a Folder Link into the Favorite Links Folder

When you release the mouse button, select the **Create Shortcut Here** option and your new shortcut will appear at the bottom of the Favorite Links bar. To rearrange the links on the bar just drag them up or down the list. To remove a link that you have placed, right-click it, and click **Remove Link** on the shortcut menu. You cannot easily remove the default links though.

9

Word and the Internet

The Web has been responsible for the rapidly expanding popularity of the Internet. As you probably know, a Web site is made up of a group of Web pages, all stored on an Internet server. The Web consists of many millions of such sites, located on server computers around the globe, all of which you can access with the browser on your PC.

So the Web consists of client computers (yours and mine) and server computers handling multimedia documents with hypertext links built into them (Web pages). Client computers use browser software (such as Internet Explorer and Navigator) to view pages of these documents, one at a time. Server computers use Web server software to maintain the documents for the rest of us to access.

Creating Web Pages

It is possible to use Word 2007 to create Web pages, but it is not easy to use the program to upload them to the Internet. We only recommend you do this as a last resort.

We do not have the space (or the inclination) to cover Web site design and management here, we can only introduce some of Word's useful features. If you want more detail on Web sites generally, may we suggest you read our book *Your own Web site on the Internet* (BP433), also published by Bernard Babani (publishing) Ltd.

Saving as a Web Page

You can use Word 2007 to create a Web page in the same way you create a 'regular' Word document, by simply saving your file as an HTML (Hypertext Markup Language) file.

The example below is an opening page for a Web site prepared as a normal **.docx** file in Word 2007.

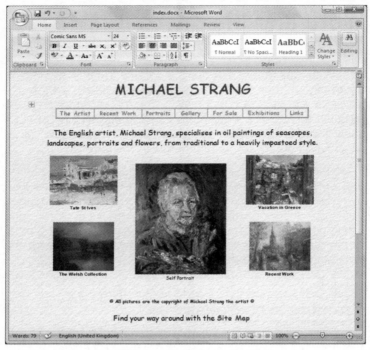

Fig. 9.1 A Web Page Created in Word

Note that it is shown in Web Layout View, controlled by the buttons on the bottom scroll bar. With this view, Word attempts to show the document as it will appear on the Web.

To save an existing, or newly created, document as a Web page, click the **Office Button** , **Save As**, **Other Formats** buttons to open the Save As dialogue box shown in Fig. 9.2. Locate the folder you want to use and in the **File name** box, type a name for the Web page. In the **Save as type** box select **Web page (*.htm, *.html)** option, and while the Save As box is open click the **Change Title** button and type the title you want to appear in the titlebar of the browser when the Web page is viewed. Click **OK** and then the **Save** button to complete the saving process.

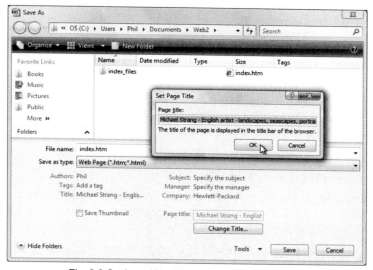

Fig. 9.2 Saving a Word Document as a Web Page

When you save a document as a Web page, all its graphics and objects are saved in a separate folder, as shown above. Here we saved the file as **index.htm** and the separate folder **index_files** was created as well. When you later reopen the Web page in Microsoft Word, the graphics and objects you see are in their original formats so that you can edit them as normal.

Some HTML Differences

As we have seen, Word 2007 automatically converts Word's **.docx** file format to HTML when creating Web pages, and back to **.docx** format when the files are loaded into the word processor. This conversion process is fairly accurate, but by no means perfect because of the basic restrictions inherent in HTML.

With HTML you cannot embed fonts and you have to use tables to control the layout of complex pages. Without them HTML will not let you simulate multiple column layouts, or very specific spacings of text blocks.

Because Word provides formatting options far more powerful than that of most Web browsers, some text and graphics may look different when you view them on a Web page. We suggest that when creating documents for the Web with Word you use the Web Layout view from scratch. This will help to ensure that your graphics look the way you want them to when they are viewed in a Web browser.

The HTML File Format

Most Web pages are still written in HTML, which can be used by Web browsers on any operating system, such as Windows, Macintosh, or UNIX.

HTML pages are actually text documents which use short codes, or tags, to control text, designate graphical elements and hypertext links. Clicking a link on a Web page brings a document located on your hard disc, a local Intranet, or on a distant Internet server to your screen, irrespective of the server's geographic location. Documents may contain text, images, sounds, movies, or a combination of these, in other words – multimedia. All of these are 'built into' a Web page with HTML code.

As we have seen, documents created in Word 2007 can also use the HTML format. Most Windows application programs save their files, or data documents, in a proprietary binary format, which can only be read by the program itself. Word 2007, uses the .docx file format as the 'main' file saving format. Word documents can also be saved in HTML as an alternative file format, and the document can still be updated and edited using all of Word's extensive formatting tools.

This means that not only can Word 2007 documents now be published as 'instant' Web pages, but they can also be sent to other people, in a workgroup for example, who can read them in their Web browsers if they don't have a copy of Word on their computer. Microsoft Office has actually made HTML into a 'universal' file format, its application files being instantly readable by anyone with a normal Web browser.

To do this, extensive use is made of 'style sheets', and the downside is that the default HTML code produced by Word is far too complex and convoluted for most Web authors to edit manually. Our example below shows only a quarter of the code produced for a document of only four lines of text. HTML documents produced this way can only really be edited in the original application itself.

```
p.MsoBodyText, li.MsoBodyText, div.MsoBodyText { mso-pagination: widow-orphan; fc
                font-family: Times New Roman; mso-fareast-font-family:
                Times New Roman; margin-left: 0cm; margin-right: 0cm;
                margin-top: 0cm; margin-bottom: .0001pt }
@page Section1
        {size:612.0pt 792.0pt;
        margin:72.0pt 90.0pt 72.0pt 90.0pt;
        mso-header-margin:36.0pt;
        mso-footer-margin:36.0pt;
        mso-paper-source:0;}
div.Section1 { page: Section1 }
-->
</style>
</head>

<body lang="EN-GB" style="tab-interval:36.0pt">

<div class="Section1">
    <p class="MsoBodyText"><b><i><span style="font-size:20.0pt;mso-bidi-font-size:
10.0pt">The Seagull<o:p></o:p></span></i></b></p>
    <p class="MsoBodyText"><span style="font-size:14.0pt;mso-bidi-font-size:10.0pt"
    seagull lies dead near the breaking waves.<b> </b>Stranded in death on the
    rocks and pebbles that lay strewn on the beach, each one appearing to me as a
    jewel of exquisite beauty.<span style="mso-spacerun: yes">  </span>The
    red coloured seaweed near the bird's head like a bloodstained pillow for its
    downy head. <o:p></o:p></span></p>
    <p class="MsoNormal"><![if !supportEmptyParas]> <![endif]><o:p></o:p></p>
</div>
<div style="mso-element:comment-list">
    <![if !supportAnnotations]>

    <hr class="msocomoff" align="left" size="1" width="33%">

    <![endif]>
</div>

</body>

</html>
```

Fig. 9.3 An Example of Word-generated HTML Code

In an effort to try to solve this problem, Word 2007 can also save files in a filtered HTML output which removes the custom code needed to maintain the file's editability. You choose the **Web Page, Filtered** in the **Save as type** option list of the **Save As** dialogue box.

Web pages saved in this format will no longer be editable in Word, but their file size is much smaller, which is important for Web transmissions. It is now much easier to use Word files, or parts of them, in other dedicated Web page development packages.

Uploading to an FTP Site

To save your Web page to the Internet (so that other people can access it) you need to have access to server space. This is usually provided free by broadband or e-mail providers, and you should have FTP (or file transfer) access to this space on the server. Once you have the access details from your System Administrator and before you can save any files to an FTP site with Word 2007, you must tell Word where to look for the site.

You do this from the Save As dialogue box, (Fig. 9.2), by clicking the **Tools** button and selecting the **Map Network Drive** option. This opens the box shown earlier in Fig. 8.13, in which you select the **Connect to a Web site that you can use to store your documents and pictures** link to open the Add Network Location wizard shown below.

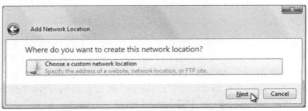

Fig. 9.4 Adding an FTP Network Location

In the various boxes that open, type the FTP site name given to you by your ISP. This could be a series of numbers separated by dots, or a URL in the form:

ftp:/ftp.servername.com

If you have user privileges for the site, enter your user name and your password when you are asked for it, as well as the name you wish to call the location on your PC. You should then see something like we show in Fig. 9.5 below.

Fig. 9.5 The Network Location Successfully Created

Clicking the **Finish** button closes the wizard and opens a window showing the new location.

To save a Web page file from Word to your FTP site, and hence make it available over the Internet, first make sure your Internet connection is open. Then click the **Office Button** , **Save As**, **Other Formats** buttons and in the **Save As** dialogue box, double-click the **Computer** item in the Favorite Links list in the navigation Pane on the left. Your FTP site should now appear in the main pane of the dialogue box, for you to select as the saving location.

Double-clicking this should make the connection to your Web server space, and present you with the list of folders and files that are there. Double-click the location at the site you want, type the document name, in the **Save as type** box select the **Web page (*.htm, *.html)** option and click the **Save** button to, hopefully, complete the operation.

In the future, if you need to edit or update a Web page, you can use the Open dialogue box to retrieve the file from your Web server. Once you have carried out your work you can save it back again as described above.

This procedure is fine for one off pages, or very small Web sites, but not for sites of more than a few pages.

Web Archive Files

You can also save your Web page as a Web archive **.mht** file so that all the text and graphics are stored embedded in a single file. To do this, select **Single File Web Page** as the **Save as type** in the Save As dialogue box.

Blogging in Word 2007

Perhaps of more use to most people is the ability of Word 2007 to very easily send postings to your personal blog. A blog is a special Web site a little like a very public personal diary, but you can use it however you want to. You make entries, or postings, on an ongoing basis, with the latest appearing at the top, so your visitors can read what's new. They can then make comments, link to it, or e-mail you. But only if they are interested in your material!

Blogging by politicians and other 'high profile' personalities, to express opinions on such things as the wars in Iraq and Afghanistan, for example, have proved the role of blogs as a news source. In fact, over the last few years, blogs have reshaped the Web, enabling millions of people to have an international voice and connect with others.

We haven't had much time ourselves to get too involved with our own blogs, but have gone through the procedure of setting one up and sending to it, to demonstrate the usefulness of Word 2007. Maybe we will get more active later.

Setting Up a Blog

To start blogging in Word 2007, you first have to create a blog account with a service provider (we list some below). Once that is done, Word has to be configured to use your account information when you open or publish blog posts.

If you don't have an account with a blog provider, you could try one of the following free providers which all work well with Word.

WordPress	http://www.wordpress.com
Blogger	http://www.blogger.com
Windows Live Spaces	http://spaces.live.com

We set up our account with Blogger, which is part of the Google empire. This was very easy. We just logged onto the Web address given above, created an account, named the blog, and chose a template for it. In just five minutes we had our own empty blog with the exciting name of Phil Oliver.

Before going back to Word 2007 you will need to make a note of the **User Name** and **Password** that lets you access the blog.

Registering the Blog in Word

Now you have your blog you must first register it in Word, so that it will be automatically accessed whenever you make a posting. Click the **Office Button** , followed by the **Publish**, **Blog** buttons to open the Register a Blog Account dialogue box shown here in Fig. 9.6. To open the Blog Registration Wizard, click the **Register Now** button in this box. You then have to work through a series of dialogue boxes entering information about your blog.

Fig. 9.6 Opening the Blog
Registration Wizard

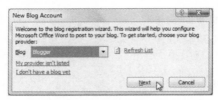

Fig. 9.7 Entering the Blog Provider

In the first box shown in Fig. 9.7, you select your Blog provider. If you have set one up with a service provider that Word already knows about, just select it from the **Blog** list and click the **Next** button. Then enter your **User Name**, and **Password** in the next box and click on **OK**.

If your provider is not on the list, you can set up a custom account as long as your service supports the 'metaweblog' or 'Atom' type of API (short for Application Programming Interface). If so, in the New Blog Account dialogue box (Fig. 9.7 above), select **Other** in the **Blog** list, and click the **Next** button. Then in the New Account dialogue box that opens, select your **API**, and type your **Blog Post URL**, your **User Name**, and your **Password**. If you don't know any of these check with your provider.

Hopefully the next box opened will be the last, as shown in Fig. 9.8. You are now set up to blog from Word.

Fig. 9.8 A Successful Blog Registration

The Blog Window

You can start a new blog entry by simply clicking the **Office Button** 🔘, then the **New** button and selecting **New blog post** in the New Document window. Or, if you want to start your posting from an existing document, click the **Office Button** 🔘, followed by the **Publish**, **Blog** buttons.

Fig. 9.9 Word 2007 in Blogging Mode

The Blog Post window, as shown above, has only two tabs, **Blog Post** and **Insert**. The **Blog Post** tab provides the tools for working, with your **Blog**, with the **Clipboard**, for entering **Basic Text**, applying **Styles** to it, and finally for **Proofing** your entry. The **Insert** tab lets you add such things as **Tables**, **Illustrations**, hypertext **Links**, WordArt **Text** and **Symbols**. Some of these may only work if your blog service provider lets you include images in your blogs, in which case you may have to arrange online storage for them.

Creating a Blog Posting

Before you begin entering text for your post, click in the **[Enter Post Title Here]** prompt and type the title for your blog entry. Then click below the line to begin entering the body text for your posting.

When you have finished, click the **Blog Post**, **Proofing**, **Spelling** button to make sure you have no spelling mistakes. You can also change the formatting of the text with the **Blog Post**, **Basic Text** command buttons, the same as you would in any other Word document. To change the style of the text, use the options in the **Styles** gallery. Actually it is better to just use the styles, as more complicated text editing is quite likely to be thrown away when you post!

Fig. 9.10 The Insert Ribbon

The **Insert** tab, shown in Fig. 9.10 above, lets you add graphics and other features to your blog in the same way as we have described in other parts of the book. We suggest you use them sparingly, as blogs are better kept simple. As long as you have arranged suitable storage space, Word will take care of uploading any pictures that you insert in the blog post, and will even automatically generate **.png** files for any Office graphics, like charts or diagrams. Very clever.

If you want to archive your postings, just **Save** them as you would any other Word document. When you re-open them in the future, Word will remember that they are blog posts and will set the Ribbon accordingly. This means that you can open posts later and make changes without visiting your blog's 'admin' panel.

Sending a Posting

When you are finished, click the **Blog Post**, **Blog**, **Publish** button, shown here. Your posting will be uploaded to your blog site and should show at the top of the list of posts. To check, just click the **Home Page** button (in the **Blog** group) which will open your blog in your default browser, probably Explorer. The other buttons in the **Blog** group let you access and manage your blog service accounts.

This is an excellent feature of Word 2007. You can do all your blogging without being connected to your blog site, and can use an editor (Word) that you are well used to, instead of the one provided on the site. No longer will you get 'time out' errors because you have been logged on too long while composing your missive.

Using Hypertext Links

Hypertext links are elements in a blog, document or Web page that you can click with your mouse, to 'jump to' another document. When clicked they actually fetch another file, or part of a file, to your screen, and the link is the address that uniquely identifies the location of the target file, whether it is located on your PC, on an Intranet, or on the Internet itself. This address is known as a Uniform Resource Locator (URL for short). For a link to an Internet file to work you must obviously have access to the Internet from your PC.

Inserting a Hyperlink

If you know the URL address of the link destination, you can simply type it in a Word document and it will be automatically 'formatted' as a hyperlink by Word. This usually means it will change to bright blue underlined text, as shown below.

The URL for my Web site is http://www.philoliver.com

Fig. 9.11 An Automatically Generated Hyperlink

If you don't want to create a hyperlink from the text, just right-click it and select the **Remove Hyperlink** option. This feature can sometimes get annoying but you can turn it off if you want. To do this, click the Microsoft Office button, select **Word Options**, **Proofing**, **AutoCorrect Options**, and in the **AutoFormat As You Type** tab clear the **Internet and network paths with hyperlinks** check box.

In Word a hyperlink consists of the text, or image, that the user sees that describes the link, the URL of the link's target, and a ScreenTip (with an instruction) that appears whenever the pointer passes over the link on the screen.

To insert a manual hyperlink into Word, select the display text or image, and either click the **Insert**, **Links**, **Hyperlink** button Hyperlink, or use the **Ctrl+K** keyboard shortcut. They both open the Insert Hyperlink dialogue box.

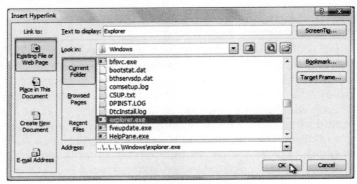

Fig. 9.12 The Insert Hyperlink Box

To illustrate the procedure, start Word, open the **PC Users4** memo, and highlight the word 'Explorer' to be found towards the end of it. Next, click the **Insert**, **Links**, **Hyperlink** button and locate the **explorer.exe** file (in the **Windows** folder of your PC) using the **Look in** list, as shown above.

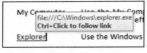

Fig. 9.13 A Hyperlink

Pressing the **OK** button, underlines the highlighted text and changes its colour to blue. When you point to such a hyperlink, a message opens, as shown here in Fig. 9.13. We did not place a ScreenTip so the link address is shown instead. In our case, left-clicking the link with the **Ctrl** key depressed, starts Explorer. When you have finished using Explorer, click its **Close** button for the program to return you automatically to the hyperlinked Word document.

Inserting an Internet Hyperlink

To insert an Internet hyperlink into Word, select the display text or image, and click the **Insert**, **Links**, **Hyperlink** button to open the Insert Hyperlink dialogue box shown again in Fig. 9.14 on the next page.

Fig. 9.14 Linking to a Web Page

To place an Internet hyperlink, click **Existing File or Web Page** on the 'Link to' bar and if necessary enter the hyperlink text in the **Text to display** box. Specify the linked document by either typing its URL in the **Address** box, as shown above, or choosing from the **Recent Files** or **Browsed Pages** file lists. You could also click the **Browse the Web** button in the dialogue box and find the page to link to on the Internet.

Next, click **ScreenTip** to create a ScreenTip that will be displayed whenever the mouse pointer moves over the hyperlink. Clicking **OK** twice will place the link onto your document. Our example above placed the link shown here in Fig. 9.15.

Fig. 9.15 A Hyperlink Screen Tip

Clicking this link with the **Ctrl** key depressed opened our Web browser in a new window and loaded the linked Web site into it.

Inserting Other Hyperlinks

There are three other types of hyperlinks you can place from the Insert Hyperlink box, shown by the other buttons on the **Link to** bar.

To link to a location in the same Word file, click the **Place in This Document** button. Before doing this, though, you should place a bookmark at the link location with the **Insert**, **Links**, **Bookmark** command button, so that you have somewhere to 'jump to'.

To link to a document not yet created, click the **Create New Document** button and enter the name for the new Word file. You can then edit the new file when convenient.

To create a link to an **E-mail Address**, either type the e-mail address you want in the **E-mail address** box, or select from the **Recently used e-mail addresses** box. In the **Subject** box, type the subject of the e-mail message. Word will create a new e-mail message with the address already placed in the **To** line and a title in the **Subject** line of the message header, when the hyperlink is activated.

Word uses 'mailto' followed by the e-mail address and the subject line as the tip if you do not specify one. This type of link is usually used when you want to make it easy for people to contact you.

Drag-and-drop Hyperlinks

You can also create a hyperlink by dragging selected text or a graphic from another Word document, a PowerPoint slide, a range in Excel, or a selected Access database object to your Word document. Both documents need to be saved as files before this will work. Use the right mouse button to drag the selection to your document, release the mouse button and select **Create Hyperlink Here** from the shortcut menu.

Editing Hyperlinks

Once a hyperlink has been placed in a Word document it is very easy to change by right-clicking on it and selecting **Edit Hyperlink** from the drop-down menu. This opens a similar dialogue box to that used for inserting the link in the first place. You can make any changes you like in this box.

10

Sharing Information

Office 2007 is the most integrated suite to come from the Microsoft stables. The new Themes feature makes it easy to keep consistent colours, fonts, and special effects between your Word 2007, Excel 2007, and PowerPoint 2007 documents, and Office Styles help ensure a consistent appearance among the diagrams, tables, and shapes.

The improved charting capabilities in Excel 2007 are shared across the main Office programs, so you can create and interact with charts the same way, whichever program you are using. You can build tables and charts in PowerPoint 2007 with the same tools you use in Excel and Word 2007. You can create SmartArt graphics in Word, Excel, and PowerPoint documents in exactly the same way.

To transfer information between Office programs, or many other Windows programs for that matter, you copy, move, link, embed, or hyperlink information depending on the imposed situation, as follows:

Imposed Situation	*Method to Adopt*
Inserted information will not need updating.	Copy or move
Inserted information needs to be automatically updated in the destination file as changes are made to the data in the source file, or Source file will always be available and you want to minimise the size of your file.	Link
Source file not always accessible, or Destination file needs to be edited without the changes showing in the source file.	Embed
To jump to a location in a document or Web page, or to a file in a different program.	Hyperlink

Copying or Moving Information

To copy or move information between Office 2007 programs is extremely easy. Most of the time you can just drag and drop a selection between programs. It is safer to do this with the right mouse button depressed, as you are usually given the option to **Move** or **Copy**. This prevents you actually deleting something from the source document, when you only wanted to copy it.

To illustrate the technique, we will copy the **Project3.xlsx** file, created in Excel, into a Word document. Let's first assume that we only have the source file **Project3.xlsx** on disc, and don't have Excel on the computer. In such a situation, you can only copy the whole file to the destination program, Word 2007.

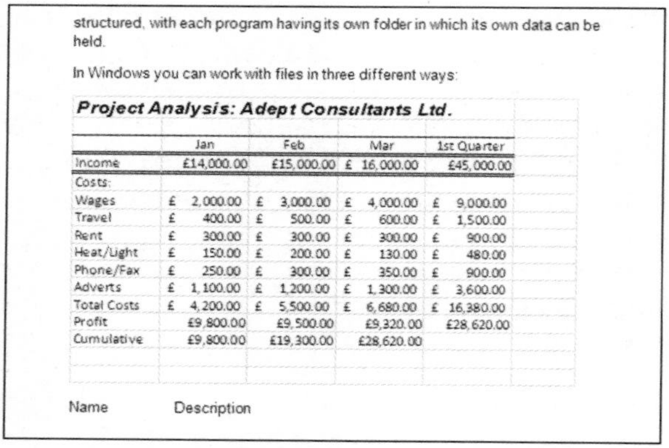

structured, with each program having its own folder in which its own data can be held.

In Windows you can work with files in three different ways:

Project Analysis: Adept Consultants Ltd.

	Jan	Feb	Mar	1st Quarter
Income	£14,000.00	£15,000.00	£ 16,000.00	£45,000.00
Costs:				
Wages	£ 2,000.00	£ 3,000.00	£ 4,000.00	£ 9,000.00
Travel	£ 400.00	£ 500.00	£ 600.00	£ 1,500.00
Rent	£ 300.00	£ 300.00	£ 300.00	£ 900.00
Heat/Light	£ 150.00	£ 200.00	£ 130.00	£ 480.00
Phone/Fax	£ 250.00	£ 300.00	£ 350.00	£ 900.00
Adverts	£ 1,100.00	£ 1,200.00	£ 1,300.00	£ 3,600.00
Total Costs	£ 4,200.00	£ 5,500.00	£ 6,680.00	£ 16,380.00
Profit	£9,800.00	£9,500.00	£9,320.00	£28,620.00
Cumulative	£9,800.00	£19,300.00	£28,620.00	

Name   Description

Fig. 10.1 A Copied Spreadsheet in Word 2007

To achieve this, do the following:

- Start Word and minimise it on the Taskbar.

- Use Computer (or Explorer) to locate the file whose contents you want to copy into Word.

- Click the filename that you want to copy, hold the mouse button down and point to Word on the Taskbar until the application opens.

- While still holding the mouse button down, move the mouse pointer into Word's open document to where you want to insert the contents of **Project3.xlsx**.

- Release the mouse button to place the contents of the Excel file into Word at that point.

Source File and Application Available

If you have Office 2007 installed you should have both Excel and Word on your PC, so you should have both the file and the application that created it on your computer. You can then copy all or part of the contents of the source file to the destination file, as follows:

- Start Excel and open **Project3.xlsx**, select the information to copy and click the **Home**, **Clipboard**, **Copy** button.

- Start Word, locate where you want the insertion and click the **Home**, **Clipboard**, **Paste** button. Then select the first **Keep Source Formatting** option from the menu that opens when you click the Paste Options Smart Tag, as shown in Fig. 10.2 below.

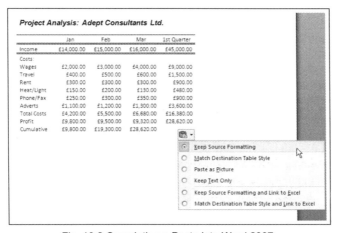

Fig. 10.2 Completing a Paste into Word 2007

If you are wondering how we managed to get the £ signs to display at the beginning of the numbers, instead of to the left of the Excel column (the default for currency format), we changed the format of the cell. In Excel, we selected the cells involved, clicked the **Dialogue Box Launcher** on the **Number** group of the **Home** tab, selected **Custom** in the **Category** list, and chose one of the three **£#,##..** options as shown below in Fig. 10.3. This shows the result as well.

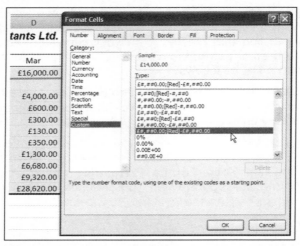

Fig. 10.3 Setting a Custom Currency Format in Excel 2007

Object Linking and Embedding

Object Linking is copying information from one file (the source file) to another file (the destination file) and maintaining a connection between the two files. When information in the source file is changed, then the information in the destination file is automatically updated. Linked data is stored in the source file, while the file into which you place the data stores only the location of the source and displays a representation of the linked data.

For example, you would use Linking if you wanted an Excel chart included in a Word document to be updated whenever the data in Excel was changed. The Excel worksheet containing the chart would be referred to as the source file, while the Word document would be referred to as the destination file.

Object Embedding is inserting information created in one file (the source file) into another file (the container file). After it is embedded, the object becomes part of the container file. When you double-click an embedded object, it opens in the application in which it was created in the first place. You can then edit it in place, and the original object in the source application remains unchanged.

Thus, the main differences between linking and embedding are where the data is stored and how it is updated after you place it in your file. Linking saves you disc space as only one copy of the linked object is kept on disc. Embedding a logo in the Word template used for your headed paper, would save the logo every time a letter was saved, whereas linking it would not.

Linking Selected Information

To link selected information from an existing file created in one application into another, do the following:

- Select the information in the source file you want to link and click the **Home**, **Clipboard**, **Copy** button, or the **Ctrl+C** shortcut.

- In the destination file, locate where you want the insertion placed and click the **Home**, **Clipboard**, **Paste** button. Then select the first **Keep Source Formatting and Link to ...** option from the menu that opens when you click the Paste Options Smart Tag, as shown earlier in Fig. 10.2.

Embedding Selected Information

To embed selected information from an existing file created in one application into another, do the following:

- Select the information in the source file you want to link and click the **Home**, **Clipboard**, **Copy** button, or the **Ctrl+C** shortcut.

- In the destination file, locate where you want the insertion placed and click the **Home**, **Clipboard**, **Paste Special** button. Select the type of object involved in the **As** list as shown in Fig. 10.4, where we were embedding a selection from an Excel worksheet.

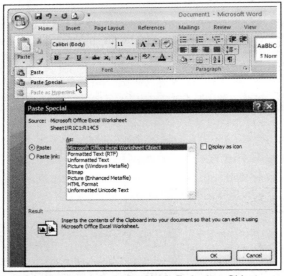

Fig. 10.4 Using Paste Special to Embed an Object

- To embed the object, make sure the **Paste** option button is selected and click **OK**.

- The **Paste link** option button gives you another way of linking the object.

- The **Display as icon** check box, places an icon, which you can double-click to open the object data in the source file application.

Sharing with Others

When you are ready to share your Word 2007 files with your friends or co-workers, there are two commands on the **Office Button** 🔵 menu for you to use. The **Send** command lets you e-mail your file or send it by an Internet fax service. The **Publish** command gives you options for posting your files to a document management server or document workspace (but both require you to use Microsoft Windows SharePoint Services).

Publish as PDF or XPS

You can download a free, add-in utility from the Microsoft Download Center that lets you save or send your files in **PDF** and **XPS** formats. These file types are saved in a paginated, finished format that others can view no matter what type of computer system they are using. This is especially useful when you want to share your work with customers or business partners or make it ready for commercial printing. You can optimise for commercial press, high-quality desktop printing, online distribution, or on-screen display.

Using Mail Merge

There are times when you may want to send the same basic letter or e-mail to several different people, or companies. The easiest way to do this is with a Mail Merge operation from Word 2007. For this to work, the basic content of all the letters or e-mail messages must be the same, the differences being specific to each recipient, such as name, address, etc. You can also use Mail Merge for the following:

Envelopes   The return address is the same on all the envelopes, but the destination address is unique on each one.

Labels   Each label shows a person's unique name and address.

A Catalogue The same kind of information, such as name and description, is shown for each item, but the name and description in each item is unique.

Two files are prepared; a 'Data' file with the names and addresses, and a 'Form' file, containing the text and format of the letter. The two files are then merged together to produce a third file containing an individual letter to each party listed in the original data file.

Before creating a list of names and addresses for a mail merge, you need to select the Office application that is most suited to the task. For a mail merge, you can use a list you create in Access, Excel, Outlook, or Word itself.

- For a long list in which you expect to add, change, or delete records, and for which you want a powerful sorting and searching capability at your disposal, you should use either Access 2007 or Excel 2007.

- You can use your Outlook 2007 Contacts list of names and addresses.

- For a small to medium size list of names and addresses in which you do not expect to make too many changes, it is easiest to create a list in Word.

We will illustrate the merge procedure by using a memo created in Word (**PC User1**) and a table created in Word. First start Word and open the **PC User1** memo (or your own letter), then place two empty lines at the very top of the memo/letter by placing the insertion pointer at the beginning of the memo and pressing **Enter** twice. Then select these two empty lines and choose the Normal paragraph style.

Next, click the **Mailings**, **Start Mail Merge** button and choose the **Step by Step Mail Merge Wizard** option which opens the Mail Merge Task Pane shown in Fig. 10.5 below.

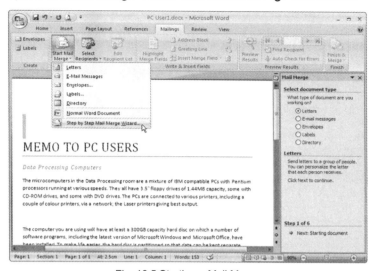

Fig. 10.5 Starting a Mail Merge

In this Task Pane, you define:

1. The document type to be used.

2. Whether to use the current document.

3. The source of your data – create a new list or use an existing one.

4. Write your letter if not already written, and select type of insert (such as Address block or Greeting line).

5. Preview your letters.

6. Complete merge by printing or editing individual letters.

In what follows, we will examine each of these steps. You can, of course, skip the Create an Address List in Word section, if you already have an existing data list.

Creating an Address List in Word

On the third **Mail Merge** Task Pane option, click the **Type a new list** option button, then click the **Create** link. In the displayed New Address List box, click the **Customize Columns** button to display the Customize Address List box shown in Fig. 10.6 below.

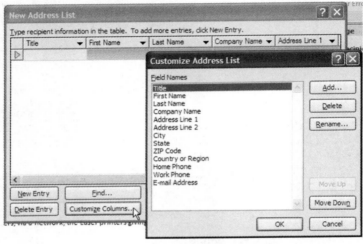

Fig. 10.6 The Customize Address List Box

As you can see, Word provides commonly used field names for your address list. Unwanted field names can be deleted from the list by selecting them and pressing the **Delete** button. To add your own field name, click the **Add** button and supply details in the displayed dialogue box. The **Move** buttons can be used to move a selected field in the list up or down. Finally, an existing field name can be renamed by highlighting it then pressing the **Rename** button and supplying a different name.

Having compiled the required field names for your list, press the **OK** button to display the New Address List box, shown in Fig. 10.7 in which you can add the names and other details of your contacts.

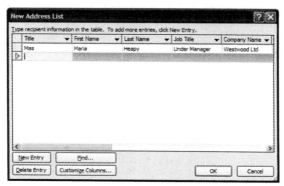

Fig. 10.7 Adding Addresses to the New Address List Box

Having completed your list, click the **OK** button which displays the Save Address List dialogue box, shown in Fig. 10.8, for you to name your data list, say **Customers**; Word adds the file extension **.mdb**.

Fig. 10.8 The Save Address List Dialogue Box

Now click the **Next** link at the bottom of the **Mail Merge** Task Pane to go to the fourth step in which you can click the **Address block** link to display the Insert Address Block box shown in Fig. 10.9. This is where you choose the way the recipient's address will display in your letter or memo.

If you have renamed fields or are using an external data file that does not contain the exact default fields displayed in Fig. 10.6, you will need to click the **Match Fields** button in

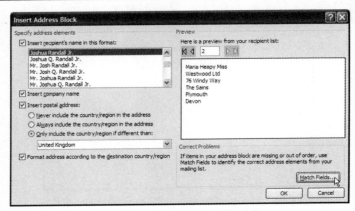

Fig. 10.9 The Insert Address Block Box

the Insert Address Block box of Fig. 10.9 to open the Match Fields box shown in Fig. 10.10 below.

Fig. 10.10 Matching Merge Fields

Having matched the fields from your data to the default fields, click the **OK** button on each opened dialogue box to get back to the 'Form' file, containing the text and format of the letter in Word 2007.

Selecting the entry **<<<<AddressBlock>>>>** at the top of the letter, then right-clicking displays a drop-down menu with options to **Edit Address Block** or **Toggle Field Codes**, to mention but a few. The placed codes are shown in Fig. 10.11 below.

{ ADDRESSBLOCK \f "<<_FIRST0_>><<_LAST0_>><<_SUFFIX0_>>
<<_COMPANY_
>><<_STREET1_
>><<_STREET2_
>><<_CITY_
>><<_STATE_
>><<_POSTAL_>><<
COUNTRY>>" \l 2057 \c 2 \e "United Kingdom" \d }

MEMO TO PC USERS

Data Processing Computers

By studying the codes of the first four lines you can soon find out how the data information is placed. If you leave these codes as they are, going to the fifth step of

Fig. 10.11 Address Block Field

the **Mail Merge** Task Pane displays the recipient's address at the top of your letter as shown in Fig. 10.12.

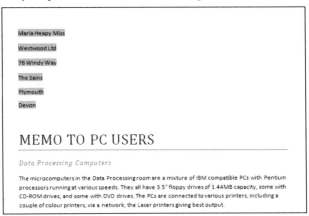

Fig. 10.12 Preview of the Merged Letter

The last step in the **Mail Merge** Task Pane allows you to print all your letters or edit individual ones. That's all there is to it. You will possibly find it takes as little time to do, as it did to read about!

11

Customising Word 2007

Word Macro Basics

A macro is simply a set of instructions made up of a sequence of keystrokes, mouse selections, or commands stored in a macro file. After saving, or writing, a macro and attaching a quick key combination to it, you can run the same sequence of commands whenever you want. This can save a lot of time and, especially with repetitive operations, can save mistakes creeping into your work.

In Word there are two basic ways of creating macros. The first one is generated by the program itself, recording and saving a series of keystrokes, or mouse clicks. The second one involves using Visual Basic for Applications, the programming language that is common to all Office applications. With this method, you can write quite complex macro programs directly into a macro file using the Visual Basic Editor.

To work with macros in Word 2007, you need to have the Developer tab showing on the Ribbon, so click the **Office Button** , then click **Word Options**, in the **Popular** tab select the **Show Developer tab in the Ribbon** check box, as shown in Fig. 11.1.

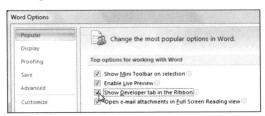

Fig. 11.1 Enabling the Developer Tab in the Ribbon

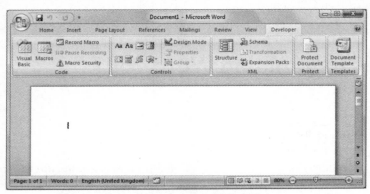

Fig. 11.2 The Developer Ribbon Tab

Recording a Macro

To demonstrate how easy it is to save and name a macro, we will start with a simplistic one that enhances the word at the cursor to bold italics type. Open a document, place the cursor in a word and either click the **Macro** indicator on the Status bar, shown here, or click the **Developer**, **Code**, **Record Macro** button .

Fig. 11.3 The Record Macro Dialogue Box

Either of these, opens the Record Macro dialogue box shown in Fig. 11.3. In the **Macro name** input box, type a name for your macro (call it BoldItalic), then give your macro a **Description** (such as Bold & Italic) and click on the **Keyboard** button.

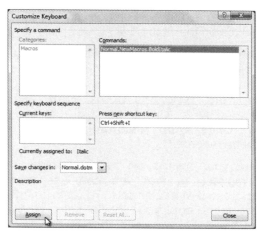

Fig. 11.4 Adding Keyboard Commands to a Macro

In the displayed Customize Keyboard dialogue box, shown in Fig. 11.4, press a suitable key stroke combination, such as **Ctrl+Shift+I**, in the **Press new shortcut key** input box.

You will be informed whether this key combination is currently attached to an internal macro or not, as shown in Fig. 11.4.

Most **Ctrl**, or **Shift** keys with a letter or function key combinations are suitable (the word [unassigned] will appear under the **Currently assigned to:** heading) if the chosen combination of keys is not already assigned to a macro. Our choice of key strokes results in the message 'Italic', under the **Currently assigned to:** heading. This does not matter in this instance, because both the key combinations **Ctrl+I** and **Ctrl+Shift+I** are assigned to Italic, so we can use one.

Next, press the **Assign** button followed by the **Close** button. From this point on, all key strokes and mouse control clicks (but not mouse movements or text selections) will be recorded. To indicate that the recorder is on, Word attaches a recorder graphic to the mouse pointer, as shown here. Word also displays the **Stop Recording** and **Pause Recording** buttons in the **Code** group on the **Developer** Ribbon tab.

A macro can also be stopped by clicking the **Macro** button on the Status bar.

While the cursor is still placed in the word to be modified, use the key strokes, **Ctrl+⇨** to move to the end of the current word followed by **Shift+Ctrl+⇦** to highlight it, click the **Home**, **Font**, **Bold** and **Home**, **Font**, **Italic** buttons, press the **⇨** key to cancel the highlight and click the **Developer**, **Code**, **Stop Recording** button. Your macro should now be recorded.

By default your macros will be incorporated into Word's Normal template, so that you can use them in any documents created at a later date. To restrict a macro to the current document only you should select the document filename in the **Store macro in** box of the Record Macro dialogue box (Fig. 11.3).

Playing Back a Macro

There are three main ways of running a macro. You can use the playback shortcut keys straight from the keyboard; in our case place the cursor in another word and press the **Ctrl+Shift+I** keys. The word should be enhanced automatically. If not, check back that you carried out the instructions correctly.

The second method is to click the **Developer**, **Code**, **Macros** button, or use the **Alt+F8** keyboard shortcut, then select the macro from the list in the Macros dialogue box, as shown below, and press the **Run** button.

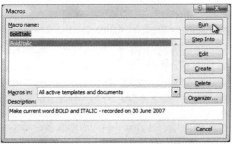

Fig. 11.5 Running a Macro from the Macros Dialogue Box

From this dialogue box you can also **Edit**, **Create** or **Delete** macros, or select the **Organizer** which allows you to copy macro sets between the document and the Normal template.

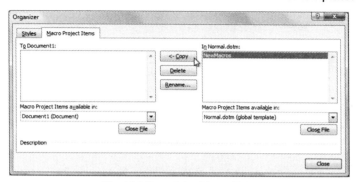

Fig. 11.6 Organising Macro Sets

Attaching a Macro to the Toolbar

The last method of activating a macro is to attach it to a custom button on the Quick Access Toolbar (page 29) and then simply to click this button.

To assign the macro to the Quick Access Toolbar, click the **Developer**, **Code**, **Record Macro** button [Record Macro] to open the Record Macro dialogue box shown in Fig. 11.3. In the **Macro name** input box, type a name for your macro, give it a **Description** and click on the **Button** icon. This opens the Word Options dialogue box in the **Customize the Quick Access Toolbar...** section, as shown in Fig. 11.7 on the next page.

In the **Customize Quick Access Toolbar** selection box, select the document (or all documents) for which you want the macro to be available on the Toolbar.

Under **Choose commands from**, click the macro that you are recording, and then click **Add** to add it to the Toolbar section in the right-hand pane. To change the new button's image and its display name, click the **Modify** button and make what changes you want in the Modify Button box, shown open in Fig. 11.7.

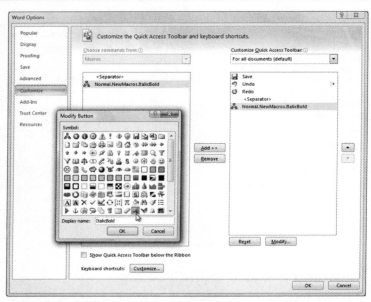

Fig. 11.7 Assigning a Macro to the Quick Access Toolbar

Clicking **OK** twice will begin recording the macro, and all key strokes and mouse control clicks (but not mouse movements or text selections) will be recorded. As before, step through the process you want recorded and then click the **Stop Recording** button.

Fig. 11.8 The New Quick Access Button

Your new macro should be recorded and a new button should have been placed on the Quick Access Toolbar, like ours shown here. Even the screen tip works when you move the pointer over it!

To remove a macro button from a toolbar, right-click it and select the **Remove from Quick Access Toolbar** menu option. You will still have to use the **Delete** button in the Macros dialogue box (Fig. 11.5) to remove the actual macro though.

Editing a Macro

You can edit the entries in a macro file by clicking the **Developer**, **Code**, **Macros** button, or using the **Alt+F8** keyboard shortcut, to open the Macros dialogue box, shown in Fig. 11.5. Select the macro from the list and press the **Edit** button. This opens the Microsoft Visual Basic for Applications Editor with the macro contents open for editing. The listing of our BoldItalic macro should look like that in Fig. 11.9 below.

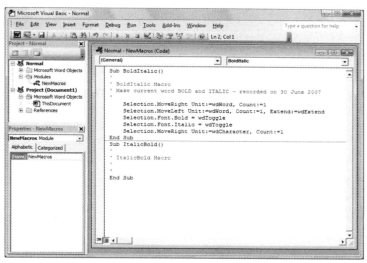

Fig. 11.9 The Visual Basic for Applications Window

If you look at this listing you will see that it would be very easy to edit the commands in the file. If you do edit it, you should then save the file with the **File**, **Save Normal** command, or **Ctrl+S**.

Macros within Visual Basic are considered to be 'subroutines' that run under an Office application, Word 2007 in this case.

It is easy to make small changes to macros you have recorded using the Visual Basic for Applications Editor. However, if you wanted to create a macro that executed commands which could not be recorded, such as switching to a particular folder and displaying the Open dialogue box, then you must learn to use the Visual Basic programming language itself. That is something that is beyond the scope of this book. You could try another of our books *Using Visual Basic* (BP498) also published by Bernard Babani (publishing) Ltd. It was not written with the Applications version of Visual Basic in mind, but it may still be useful.

You can also open the Visual Basic editor by clicking the **Developer**, **Code**, **Visual Basic** button on the Word Ribbon. To return to your document from a Visual Basic screen, click the Word icon at the top-left corner of the toolbar.

Getting Help with Visual Basic

If you have installed the complete Office 2007 package, then you will have access to the full Visual Basic for Applications Help by using the **Help** menu option from the Visual Basic Editor. The opening window arrangement is shown next in Fig. 11.10.

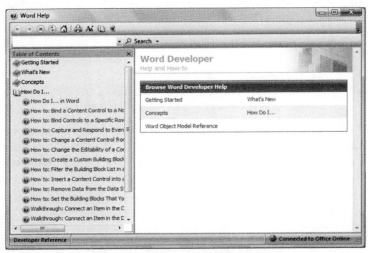

Fig. 11.10 Visual Basic and Word Developer Help

Good luck here, you might just need it!

****

That is about it. We hope you have enjoyed reading this book as much as we have enjoyed writing it. Of course Word 2007 is capable of a lot more than we have discussed here, but what we have tried to do is to give you enough information so that you can forge ahead and explore by yourself the rest of its capabilities.

An Appendix listing the available Keyboard Shortcuts in Word 2007 is included next, followed by a glossary, for reference, and in case you have trouble with any jargon that may have crept in.

Appendix
Keyboard Shortcuts

Keyboard shortcuts are single key combinations that perform a command in Word, such as **Ctrl+S** for save, or **Ctrl+B** for bold.

Key Tips on the other hand give you direct access to the Ribbon buttons, as described on page 25. When you press the **Alt** key in Word 2007, Key Tips appear in front of the Ribbon tabs and the groups and buttons on the tab. Key Tips are small indicators with a single letter or combination of letters in them, indicating what to type to activate the control under them.

Keyboard shortcuts, however, are usually the most efficient way to perform commands with the keyboard, but of course you have to be able to remember them. Hence our listing here.

The package has an incredible number of keyboard shortcuts. In the following pages we first list what we think are the most useful to remember, and then follow with the rest, divided into the different aspects of Word. The function key combinations are then listed together. We suggest you browse the listings and only attempt to memorise the shortcuts that are most useful to you.

We use here Microsoft's convention for displaying keystroke combinations. For keyboard shortcuts in which you press two or more keys at the same time, the keys to press are separated by a plus (+) sign, for example **Ctrl+P**. For keyboard shortcuts in which you press one key immediately followed by another key, the keys to press are separated by a comma (,), for example *n,* **Enter**.

Quick Reference

Shortcuts for some of the more common tasks done in a Microsoft Word 2007 document.

Ctrl+Shift+Space	Create a non-breaking space.
Ctrl+Hyphen	Create a non-breaking hyphen.
Ctrl+B	Make selected text bold.
Ctrl+I	Make selected text italic.
Ctrl+U	Underline selected text.
Ctrl+Shift+<	Decrease font size.
Ctrl+Shift+>	Increase font size.
Ctrl+]	Increase the size of text by one point.
Ctrl+[	Decrease the size of text by one point.
Ctrl+Space	Remove formatting.
Ctrl+C	Copy the selected text or object.
Ctrl+X	Cut the selected text or object.
Ctrl+V	Paste text or an object.
Ctrl+Z	Undo the last action.
Ctrl+Y	Redo the last action.
Ctrl+Alt+V	Paste special.
Ctrl+Shift+V	Paste formatting only.
Ctrl+Shift+G	Open **Word count** dialogue box.

Working with Documents

Manipulating Files

Ctrl+N	Create a new document of the same type as the current or most recent one.
Ctrl+O	Open an existing document.
Ctrl+W	Close a document.
Alt+Ctrl+S	Split the document window.
Alt+Shift+C	Remove the document window split.
Ctrl+S	Save the current document.

Finding and Replacing Text

Ctrl+F	Find text, formatting, and special items.
Alt+Ctrl+Y	Repeat a find operation, after closing the Find and Replace window.
Ctrl+H	Replace text, specific formatting, and special items.
Ctrl+G	Go to a page, bookmark, footnote, table, comment, graphic, or other location.
Alt+Ctrl+Z	Switch between the last four edits.
Alt+Ctrl+Home	Open a list of browse options.
Ctrl+Page Up	Move to previous edit location.
Ctrl+Page Dn	Move to next edit location.

Switching Views

Alt+Ctrl+P	Switch to Print Layout view.
Alt+Ctrl+O	Switch to Outline view.
Alt+Ctrl+N	Switch to Normal view.

Using Outline View

When in Outline view the following shortcuts are available.

Alt+Shift+ ⇐	Promote a paragraph.
Alt+Shift+ ⇒	Demote a paragraph.
Ctrl+Shift+N	Demote to body text.
Alt+Shift+ ⇧	Move selected paragraphs up.
Alt+Shift+ ⇩	Move selected paragraphs down.
Alt+Shift+plus (+)	Expand text under a heading.
Alt+Shift+minus (-)	Collapse text under a heading.
Alt+Shift+A	Expand or collapse all text or headings.
/ (numeric keypad)	Hide or display character formatting.
Alt+Shift+L	Show the first line of body text or all of body text.
Alt+Shift+1	Show all headings with the Heading 1 style.
Alt+Shift+n	Show all headings up to Heading n.
Ctrl+Tab	Insert a tab character.

Printing and Previewing Documents

Ctrl+P	Print a document.
Alt+Ctrl+I	Switch print preview on or off.
Arrows	Move around the preview page when zoomed in.
Page Up	Move up one preview page when zoomed out.
Page Down	Move down one preview page when zoomed out.
Ctrl+Home	Move to the first preview page when zoomed out.
Ctrl+End	Move to the last preview page when zoomed out.

Reviewing Documents

Alt+Ctrl+M	Insert a comment.
Ctrl+Shift+E	Turn track changes on or off. These show where a deletion, insertion, or other editing change has been made.
Alt+Shift+C	Close the Reviewing Pane if it is open.

Full Screen Reading View

Home	Go to beginning of document.
End	Go to end of document.
n, Enter	Go to page *n*.
Esc	Exit reading layout view.

References, Footnotes, and Endnotes

Alt+Shift+O	Mark a table of contents entry.
Alt+Shift+I	Mark a table of authorities entry.
Alt+Shift+X	Mark an index entry.
Alt+Ctrl+F	Insert a footnote.
Alt+Ctrl+D	Insert an endnote.

Working with Web Pages

Ctrl+K	Insert a hyperlink.
Alt+⇐	Go back one page.
Alt+⇒	Go forward one page.
F9	Refresh.

Navigating and Editing Text

Moving the Insertion Point

⇐	Move one character to the left.
⇒	Move one character to the right.
Ctrl+⇐	Move one word to the left.
Ctrl+⇒	Move one word to the right.
Ctrl+⇧	Move one paragraph up.
Ctrl+⇩	Move one paragraph down.
Shift+Tab	Move one cell to the left in a table.
Tab	Move one cell to the right in a table.
⇧	Move up one line.
⇩	Move down one line.
End	Move to the end of a line.
Home	To the beginning of a line.
Alt+Ctrl+Page Up	To the top of the window.
Alt+Ctrl+Page Dn	To the end of the window.
Page Up	Scroll up one screen.
Page Dn	Scroll down one screen.
Ctrl+Page Dn	Move to the top of the next page.
Ctrl+Page Up	Move to the top of the previous page.
Ctrl+End	Move to the end of a document.
Ctrl+Home	Move to the beginning of a document.
Shift+F5	Move to a previous revision.

Deleting, Copying and Moving

Backspace	Delete one character to the left.
Ctrl+Backspace	Delete one word to the left.
Delete	Delete one character to the right.
Ctrl+Delete	Delete one word to the right.
Ctrl+X	Cut selected text to the clipboard.
Ctrl+Z	Undo the last action.

Ctrl+F3	Cut to the Spike.
Ctrl+C	Copy selection to the clipboard.
Ctrl+C, Ctrl+C	Display the Office clipboard.
Ctrl+V	Paste the clipboard contents.
Alt+Shift+R	Copy the header or footer used in the previous section of the document.

Inserting Special Characters

Ctrl+F9	Insert a field.
Shift+Enter	Insert a line break, (same paragraph).
Ctrl+Enter	Insert a page break.
Ctrl+Shift+Enter	Insert a column break.
Alt+Ctrl+minus	Insert an 'em' dash.
Ctrl+minus	Insert an 'en' dash.
Ctrl+hyphen	Insert an optional hyphen.
Ctrl+Shift+hyphen	Insert a non-breaking hyphen.
Ctrl+Shift+Space	Insert a non-breaking space.
Alt+Ctrl+C	Insert the copyright symbol.
Alt+Ctrl+R	Insert the registered trademark symbol.
Alt+Ctrl+T	Insert the trademark symbol.
Alt+Ctrl+.	Insert an ellipsis.
Ctrl+'	Insert a single opening quotation mark, when placed in front of a word.
Ctrl+'	Insert a single closing quotation mark, when placed behind a word.
Ctrl+', Shift+'	Insert double opening quotation marks, when placed in front of a word.
Ctrl+', Shift+'	Insert double closing quotation marks, when placed behind a word.

Extending a Selection

F8	Turn extend mode on.
F8, or ⇨	Select the nearest character.
Shift+F8	Reduce the size of selection.
Esc	Turn extend mode off.
Shift+⇨	Extend one character to the right.
Shift+⇐	Extend one character to the left.
Ctrl+Shift+⇨	Extend to the end of a word.
Ctrl+Shift+⇐	Extend to the beginning of a word.
Shift+End	Extend to the end of a line.
Shift+Home	Extend to the beginning of a line.
Shift+⇓	Extend one line down.
Shift+⇑	Extend one line up.
Ctrl+Shift+⇓	Extend to the end of a paragraph.
Ctrl+Shift+⇑	Extend to the beginning of a paragraph.
Shift+Pg Down	Extend one screen down.
Shift+Pg Up	Extend one screen up.
Ctrl+Shift+Home	Extend to the beginning of a document.
Ctrl+Shift+End	Extend to the end of a document.
Ctrl+A	Extend to include the entire document.
Ctrl+Shift+F8	Select a vertical block of text, and then use the arrow keys; press Esc to cancel selection mode.
F8+arrow keys	Extend a selection to a specific location in a document. Esc to cancel.

Character and Paragraph Formatting

Note that some of these do not work in Full Screen Reading mode.

Ctrl+Shift+C	Copy formatting from text.
Ctrl+Shift+V	Apply the copied formatting to text.
Ctrl+Shift+F	Activates the Font box.

Ctrl+Shift+>	Increase the font size.
Ctrl+Shift+<	Decrease the font size.
Ctrl+]	Increase the font size by 1 point.
Ctrl+[	Decrease the font size by 1 point.
Ctrl+D	Opens the Font dialogue box so you can change the formatting of characters.
Shift+F3	Change the case of letters between upper, lower and title case.
Ctrl+Shift+A	Format letters as all capitals.
Ctrl+B	Apply bold formatting.
Ctrl+U	Underline selected text.
Ctrl+Shift+W	Underline words but not spaces.
Ctrl+Shift+D	Double-underline text.
Ctrl+Shift+H	Apply hidden text formatting.
Ctrl+I	Apply italic formatting.
Ctrl+Shift+K	Format letters as small capitals.
Ctrl+=	Apply subscript formatting.
Ctrl+Shift+plus	Apply superscript formatting.
Ctrl+Space	Remove manual character formatting.
Ctrl+Shift+Q	Change the selection to the Symbol font.
Ctrl+Shift+*	Display non-printing characters.
Shift+F1	Review formatting of clicked text.
Ctrl+Shift+C	Copy formats.
Ctrl+Shift+V	Paste formats.
Ctrl+1	Set line spacing to single-space.
Ctrl+2	Set line spacing to double-space.
Ctrl+5	Set line spacing to 1.5 spacing.
Ctrl+0	Add or remove one line space preceding a paragraph.
Ctrl+E	Centre the current paragraph.
Ctrl+J	Justify the current paragraph.
Ctrl+L	Left align the current paragraph.
Ctrl+R	Right align the current paragraph.
Ctrl+M	Left indent a paragraph.
Ctrl+Shift+M	Remove a left paragraph indent.

Ctrl+T	Create a hanging indent.
Ctrl+Shift+T	Reduce a hanging indent.
Ctrl+Q	Remove paragraph formatting.
Ctrl+Shift+S	Opens the Styles task pane.
Alt+Ctrl+K	Start AutoFormat.
Ctrl+Shift+N	Apply the Normal style.
Alt+Ctrl+1	Apply the Heading 1 style.
Alt+Ctrl+2	Apply the Heading 2 style.
Alt+Ctrl+3	Apply the Heading 3 style.

Working in Word Tables

Tab	Move to the next cell in the row and select its contents.
Shift+Tab	Move to the preceding cell in a row and select its contents.
Alt+Home	Move to the first cell in a row.
Alt+End	Move to the last cell in a row.
Alt+Page Up	Move to the first cell in a column.
Alt+Page Down	Move to the last cell in a column.
⇧	Move to the previous row.
⇩	Move to the next row.
Enter	Insert a new paragraph in a cell.
Ctrl+Tab	Insert a tab character in a cell.

Using Mail Merge

To use these commands the **Mailings** tab must be open.

Alt+Shift+K	Preview a mail merge.
Alt+Shift+N	Merge a document.
Alt+Shift+M	Print the merged document.

Alt+Shift+E	Edit a mail-merge data document.
Alt+Shift+F	Insert a merge field.
Alt+Shift+D	Insert a DATE field.
Alt+Ctrl+L	Insert a LISTNUM field.
Alt+Shift+P	Insert a PAGE field.
Alt+Shift+T	Insert a TIME field.
Ctrl+F9	Insert an empty field.
Ctrl+Shift+F7	Update linked information in a Word source document.
F9	Update selected fields.
Ctrl+Shift+F9	Unlink a field.
Shift+F9	Switch between a selected field code and its result.
Alt+F9	Switch between all field codes and their results.
Alt+Shift+F9	Run GOTOBUTTON or MACROBUTTON from the field that displays the field results.
F11	Go to the next field.
Shift+F11	Go to the previous field.
Ctrl+F11	Lock a field.
Ctrl+Shift+F11	Unlock a field.

Function Key Combinations

The following listings show many of the Word keyboard shortcuts indexed by the use of the function keys.

F1	Get Help or visit Microsoft Office Online.
F2	Move text or graphics.
F4	Repeat the last action.
F5	Choose the **Go To** command.
F6	Go to the next pane or frame.
F7	Choose the **Spelling** command.
F8	Extend a selection.
F9	Update selected fields.
F10	Show Key Tips on the Ribbon.
F11	Go to the next field.
F12	Choose the **Save As** command.
Shift+F1	Start context-sensitive Help or reveal formatting.
Shift+F2	Copy text.
Shift+F3	Change the case of letters.
Shift+F4	Repeat a **Find** or **Go To** action.
Shift+F5	Move to the last change.
Shift+F6	Go to the previous pane or frame.
Shift+F7	Open the Thesaurus.
Shift+F8	Shrink a selection.
Shift+F9	Switch between a field code and its result.
Shift+F10	Display a shortcut menu.
Shift+F11	Go to the previous field.
Shift+F12	Choose the **Save** command.
Ctrl+F2	Choose the **Print Preview** command.
Ctrl+F3	Cut to the Spike.
Ctrl+F4	Close the window.
Ctrl+F6	Go to the next window.

Ctrl+F9	Insert an empty field.
Ctrl+F10	Maximise the document window.
Ctrl+F11	Lock a field.
Ctrl+F12	Choose the **Open** command.
Ctrl+Shift+F3	Insert the contents of the Spike.
Ctrl+Shift+F5	Edit a bookmark.
Ctrl+Shift+F6	Go to the previous window.
Ctrl+Shift+F7	Update linked information in a Word 2007 source document.
Ctrl+Shift+F8	Then press an arrow key to extend a selection or block.
Ctrl+Shift+F9	Unlink a field.
Ctrl+Shift+F11	Unlock a field.
Ctrl+Shift+F12	Choose the Print command.
Alt+F1	Go to the next field.
Alt+F3	Create a new Building Block.
Alt+F4	Close down Microsoft Word.
Alt+F5	Restore the program window size.
Alt+F6	Move from an open dialogue box back to the document.
Alt+F7	Find the next misspelling or grammatical error.
Alt+F8	Run a macro.
Alt+F9	Switch between all field codes and their results.
Alt+F10	Maximise the program window.
Alt+F11	Display Microsoft Visual Basic code.
Alt+Shift+F1	Go to the previous field.
Alt+Shift+F2	Choose the Save command.
Alt+Shift+F7	Display the **Research** task pane.
Alt+Shift+F9	Run GOTOBUTTON or MACROBUTTON from the field that displays the field results.

Alt+Shift+F10	Display the menu or message for a smart tag.
Ctrl+Alt+F1	Display Microsoft System Information.
Ctrl+Alt+F2	Action the **Open** command.

Glossary of Terms

ActiveX
: A set of technologies that enables software components to interact with one another in a networked environment, regardless of the language in which the components were created.

Add-in
: A mini-program which runs in conjunction with another and enhances its functionality.

Address
: A unique number or name that identifies a specific computer or user on a network.

ANSI
: American National Standards Institute. A US government organisation responsible for improving communication standards.

API
: Application programming interface is a set of routines, protocols, and tools for building software applications. Programs using an API will have similar interfaces.

Application
: Software (program) designed to carry out certain activity, such as word processing, or data management.

Applet
: A program that can be downloaded over a network and launched on the user's computer.

ASCII
: A binary code representation of a character set. The name stands

for 'American Standard Code for Information Interchange'.

Association
An identification of a filename extension to a program. This lets Windows open the program when its files are selected.

Attachment
A file that is added to an e-mail message for transmission.

Authoring
The process of creating web documents or software.

Background
An image, colour or texture which forms the background of a Web page or document.

Backup
To make a back-up copy of a file or a disc for safekeeping.

Bandwidth
The range of transmission frequencies a network can use. The greater the bandwidth the more information that can be transferred over a network.

Banner
An advertising graphic shown on a Web page.

BASIC
Beginner's All-purpose Symbolic Instruction Code – a high-level programming language.

Bitmap
A technique for managing the image displayed on a computer screen.

Blog
(Web log) a frequently updated journal-style Web site. Word 2007 supports publishing to a blog.

Bookmark
A marker inserted at a specific point in a document. Used as a target for a hypertext link, or to

enable a user to return for later reference.

Boot up

To start a computer by switching it on, which initiates a self test of its Random Access Memory (RAM), then loads the necessary system files.

Browse

A button in some Windows dialogue boxes that lets you view a list of files and folders before you make a selection. Also to view a Web page.

Browser

A program, like the Internet Explorer, that lets you view Web pages.

Bug

An error in coding or logic that causes a program to malfunction.

Building blocks

Reusable text, graphics, or other document content, stored in galleries to be used in documents.

Button

A graphic element or icon in a dialogue box or toolbar that performs a specified function.

Cache

An area of memory, or disc space, reserved for data, which speeds up downloading.

Card

A removable printed-circuit board that is plugged into a computer expansion slot.

CD-ROM

Compact Disc – Read Only Memory; an optical disc which information may be read from but not written to.

Chart	A graphical view of data that is used to visually display trends, patterns, and comparisons.
Click	To press and release a mouse button once without moving the mouse.
Client	A computer that has access to services over a computer network. The computer providing the services is a server.
Client application	A Windows application that can accept linked, or embedded, objects.
Clipart	A library of drawings or photographs that you can use in your documents or presentations.
Clipboard	A temporary storage area of memory, where text and graphics are stored with the cut and copy actions. The Office XP clipboard can store up to 24 items.
Command	An instruction given to a computer to carry out a particular action.
Configuration	A general purpose term referring to the way you have your computer set up.
Context menu	A menu that opens when you right-click the mouse button on a feature. Also called object menu.
Contextual Tabs	The tabs that appear on the Ribbon according to the type of object selected in a document.
Controls	Objects on a form, report, or data access page that display data,

perform actions, or are used for decoration.

Cookies | Files stored on your hard drive by your Web browser that hold information for it to use.

Database | A collection of data related to a particular topic or purpose.

DBMS | Database management system – A software interface between the database and the user.

Default | The command, device or option automatically chosen.

Desktop | The Windows screen working background, on which you place icons, folders, etc.

Device driver | A special file that must be loaded into memory for Windows to be able to address a specific procedure or hardware device.

Device name | A logical name used by an operating system to identify a device, such as LPT1 or COM1 for the parallel or serial printer.

Dialogue box | A window displayed on the screen to allow the user to enter information.

Dial-up Connection | A popular form of Net connection for the home user, over standard telephone lines.

Digital signature | A means for originators of a message, file, or other digitally encoded information to bind their identity to the information.

Directory	An area on disc where information relating to a group of files is kept. Also known as a folder.
Disc	A device on which you can store programs and data.
Disconnect	To detach a drive, port or computer from a shared device, or to break an Internet connection.
Document	A file produced by an application program, such as Word 2007.
.docx	New XML-based default file format used by Word 2007 for documents.
Domain	A group of devices, servers and computers on a network.
Domain Name	The name of an Internet site, for example www.michaelstrang.com, which allows you to reference Internet sites without knowing their true numerical address.
Double-click	To quickly press and release a mouse button twice.
Download	To transfer to your computer a file, or data, from another computer.
DPI	Dots Per Inch – a resolution standard for laser printers.
Drag	To move an object on the screen by pressing and holding down the left mouse button while moving the mouse.
Drive name	The letter followed by a colon which identifies a floppy or hard disc drive.

Drop-down list	A menu item that can be clicked to open extra items that can be selected.
Embedded object	Information in a document that is 'copied' from its source application. Selecting the object opens the creating application from within the document.
E-mail	Electronic Mail – A system that allows computer users to send and receive messages electronically.
FAQ	Frequently Asked Questions – A common feature on the Internet, FAQs are files of answers to commonly asked questions.
File extension	The suffix following the period in a filename. Windows uses this to identify the source application program. For example **.docx** indicates a Word 2007 file.
Filename	The name given to a file. In Windows 95 and above this can be up to 256 characters long.
Firewall	Security measures designed to protect a networked system from unauthorised access.
Floppy disc	A removable disc on which information can be stored.
Fluent interface	The new interface in Word 2007, including the Ribbon, formatting galleries, pop-up formatting bars for highlighted text, etc.
Folder	An area used to store a group of files, usually with a common link.

Font	A graphic design representing a set of characters, numbers and symbols.
FTP	File Transfer Protocol. The procedure for connecting to a remote computer and transferring files.
Function key	One of the series of 12 keys marked with the letter F and a numeral, used for specific operations.
Galleries	Collections of preformatted content in Word 2007, that you can choose from.
GIF	Graphics Interchange Format, a common standard for images on the Web.
Graphic	A picture or illustration, also called an image. Formats include GIF, JPEG, BMP, PCX, and TIFF.
Hard copy	Output on paper.
Hard disc	A device built into the computer for holding programs and data.
Hardware	The equipment that makes up a computer system, excluding the programs or software.
Help	A Windows system that gives you instructions and additional information on using a program.
Home page	The document displayed when you first open your Web browser, or the first document you come to at a Web site.

Host	Computer connected directly to the Internet that provides services to other local and/or remote computers.
HTML	HyperText Markup Language, the format used in documents on the Web.
Hyperlink	A segment of text, or an image, that refers to another document on the Web, an Intranet or your PC.
Icon	A small graphic image, or button, that represents a function or object. Clicking on an icon produces an action.
Image	See graphic.
Insertion point	A flashing bar that shows where typed text will be entered into a document.
Interface	A device that allows you to connect a computer to its peripherals.
Internet	The global system of computer networks.
Intranet	A private network inside an organisation using the same kind of software as the Internet.
IP	Internet Protocol – The rules that provide basic Internet functions.
IP Address	Internet Protocol Address – every computer on the Internet has a unique identifying number.

ISP	Internet Service Provider – A company that offers access to the Internet.
JPEG/JPG	Joint Photographic Experts Group, a popular cross-platform format for image files. JPEG is best suited for true colour original images.
Kilobyte	(KB); 1024 bytes of information or storage space.
LAN	Local Area Network – High-speed, privately-owned network covering a limited geographical area, such as an office or a building.
Laptop	A portable computer small enough to sit on your lap.
LCD	Liquid Crystal Display.
Links	The hypertext connections between Web pages.
Location	An Internet address.
Log on	To gain access to a network.
Malware	Generic term for software designed to perform harmful or surreptitious acts.
Megabyte	(MB); 1024 kilobytes of information or storage space.
Megahertz	(MHz); Speed of processor in millions of cycles per second.
Memory	Part of computer consisting of storage elements organised into addressable locations that can hold data and instructions.

Menu	A list of available options in an application.
Menu bar	The horizontal bar that lists the names of menus.
Mini Toolbar	A ghost image of available tools that appears when you select text in a Word 2007 document.
Modem	Short for Modulator-demodulator devices. An electronic device that lets computers communicate electronically.
Monitor	The display device connected to your PC, also called a screen.
Mouse	A device used to manipulate a pointer around your display and activate processes by pressing buttons.
MPEG	Motion Picture Experts Group – a video file format offering excellent quality in a relatively small file.
MS-DOS	Microsoft's implementation of the Disc Operating System for PCs.
Multimedia	The use of photographs, music and sound and movie images in a presentation.
Multi-tasking	Performing more than one operation at the same time.
Network	Two or more computers connected together to share resources.
Network server	Central computer which stores files for several linked computers.
Office Suite	A bundle of useful programs sold in one package.

OLE	Object Linking and Embedding – A technology for transferring and sharing information among software applications.
Online	Having access to the Internet.
On-line Service	Services such as America On-line and CompuServe that provide content to subscribers and usually connections to the Internet.
Operating system	Software that runs a computer.
Page	An HTML document, or Web site.
Password	A unique character string used to gain access to a network, program, or mailbox.
PATH	The location of a file in the directory tree.
PDF	Portable Document Format. A file format developed by Adobe that allows formatted pages of text and graphics to be viewed and printed correctly on any computer with a PDF Reader.
Peripheral	Any device attached to a PC.
Pixel	A picture element on screen; the smallest element that can be independently assigned colour and intensity.
Plug-and-play	Hardware which can be plugged into a PC and be used immediately without configuration.
POP3	Post Office Protocol – a method of storing and returning e-mail.

Port	The place where information goes into or out of a computer, e.g. a modem might be connected to the serial port.
ppi	Pixels per inch – A measurement of the resolution of a computer display, related to the size in inches and the total number of pixels in the horizontal and vertical directions. Often referred to as dots per inch.
Print queue	A list of print jobs waiting to be sent to a printer.
Program	A set of instructions which cause a computer to perform tasks.
Queue	A list of e-mail messages waiting to be sent over the Internet, or documents waiting to be printed.
Radio button	A method of selecting an option in an application dialogue box – also called an Option button.
RAM	Random Access Memory. The computer's volatile memory. Data held in it is lost when power is switched off.
Registered file type	File types that are tracked by the system registry and are recognised by the programs you have installed on your computer.
Research options	Reference books and research Web sites that can be accessed from Word on the Review tab.
Resource	A directory, or printer, that can be shared over a network.

Ribbon	The new tabbed interface that groups Office tools by tasks so that the ones that are used most frequently are easy to find.
Right-click	To click the right mouse button once.
ROM	Read Only Memory. A PC's non-volatile memory. Data is written into this memory at manufacture and is not affected by power loss.
RTF	Rich Text Format. An enhanced form of text that includes basic formatting and is used for transferring data between applications, or in e-mail messages.
ScreenTip	Help that appears when you hover the mouse over an element of the Ribbon.
Scroll bar	A bar that appears at the right side or bottom edge of a window.
Search	Submit a query to a search engine.
Search engine	A program that helps users find information across the Internet.
Server	A computer system that manages and delivers information for client computers.
Shared resource	Any device, program or file that is available to network users.
Site	A place on the Internet. Every Web page has a location where it resides which is called its site.

Smart tag | A button that when clicked, opens a shortcut menu to give fast access to other features or Office applications.

SMTP | Simple Mail Transfer Protocol – a protocol dictating how e-mail messages are exchanged over the Internet.

Software | The programs and instructions that control your PC.

Spamming | Sending the same message to a large number of mailing lists or newsgroups. Also to overload a Web page with excessive keywords in an attempt to get a better search ranking.

SQL | Structured Query Language, used with relational databases.

SSL | Secure Sockets Layer, the standard transmission security protocol developed by Netscape, which has been put into the public domain.

Subscribe | To become a member of.

Surfing | The process of looking around the Internet.

SVGA | Super Video Graphics Array; it has all the VGA modes but with 256, or more, colours.

Swap file | An area of your hard disc used to store temporary operating files, also known as virtual memory.

Sysop | System Operator – A person responsible for the physical operations of a computer system or network resource.

System disc — A disc containing files to enable a PC to start up.

Task bar — The bar that by default is located at the bottom of your screen whenever Windows is running. It contains the Start button, buttons for all the applications that are open, and icons for other applications.

Task Pane — A pane or sub-window that gives a range of options pertaining to the task currently being performed. New to Office XP applications.

TCP/IP — Transmission Control Protocol/Internet Protocol, combined protocols that perform the transfer of data between two computers. TCP monitors and ensures the correct transfer of data. IP receives the data, breaks it up into packets, and sends it to a network within the Internet.

Template — A page design, document, spreadsheet or database, that contains all the required formatting for a particular style or type of document.

Text file — An unformatted file of text characters saved in ASCII format.

Thumbnail — A small graphic image.

TIFF — Tag Image File Format – a popular graphic image file format.

Toggle	To turn an action on and off with the same switch.
Toolbar	A bar containing buttons or icons giving quick access to commands.
TrueType fonts	Fonts that can be scaled to any size and print as they show on the screen.
UNC	Universal Naming Convention – A convention for files that provides a machine independent means of locating the file that is particularly useful in Web based applications.
Upload/Download	The process of transferring files between computers. Files are uploaded from your computer to another and downloaded from another computer to your own.
URL	Uniform Resource Locator, the addressing system used on the Web, containing information about the method of access, the server to be accessed and the path of the file to be accessed.
User ID	The unique identifier, usually used in conjunction with a password, which identifies you on a computer.
Virus	A malicious program, downloaded from a web site, e-mail or disc, designed to wipe out information on your computer.
Watermark	Toned down image or text that appears in the background of a printed page.

WAV	Waveform Audio (**.wav**) – a common audio file format for DOS/Windows computers.
Web	A network of hypertext-based multimedia information servers. Browsers are used to view any information on the Web.
Web Page	An HTML document that is accessible on the Web.
Webmaster	One whose job it is to manage a web site.
Wizard	A Microsoft tool that shows how to perform certain operations, or asks you questions and then creates an object depending on your answers.
WordArt	A feature in Microsoft Office applications, that allows you to apply a whole range of special effects to text.
XML formats	(Extensible Markup Language) New default file formats for Office 2007 programs.
XPS	(XML Paper Specification) is Microsoft's answer to the Adobe PDF file format. It describes electronic paper in a way that can be read by hardware, software, and by humans. Microsoft has integrated XPS into Office 2007 and the Windows Vista operating system, but XPS itself is platform independent, openly published, and available royalty-free.

Index